BIG BARBEL

Bonded by the Challenge

Edited by Bob Church

Contributors: Peter Reading, Guy Robb, Ray Walton and Brian Dowling

The Crowood Press

First published in 2005 by
The Crowood Press Ltd
Ramsbury, Marlborough
Wiltshire SN8 2HR

www.crowood.com

British Library Cataloguing-in-Publication Data
A catalogue record for this book is available from the British
Library.

ISBN 1 86126 725 8

Dedication
I dedicate this book to the memory of our great friend for many
years – the late Peter Stone. Like me, he was more of an all-
rounder than just a barbel fisherman. But, also like me, the
barbel became his favourite species to fish for.

Acknowledgements
I would like to thank the various record holders, and others, who
have supplied the photographs for the book. Of course, many
thanks to my four main contributors Ray Walton, Brian Dowling,
Pete Reading and Guy Robb, they really did a great job. Finally,
to my old friend Peter Wheat, a father figure in barbel fishing
circles, who wrote the Foreword.

Typeset by Jean Cussons Typesetting, Diss, Norfolk

Printed and bound in Great Britain by CPI Bath

Contents

Foreword

Barbel fishing has changed out of all recognition as compared with how it was forty years ago. When my *Fighting Barbel* was published in 1967, it represented the collective understanding of the barbel and how to catch it at that time. Now it is just a nostalgic read for anyone wanting to know what it was all like in the early days of specimen hunting and barbel specialism.

In the 1960s, comparatively few rivers held barbel. If you wanted to be in with a chance of finding an elusive lunker of over ten pounds, it was essential to visit the Royalty Fishery at Christchurch – the *only* stretch of *any* river in the country where you might catch such a big barbel.

Now things are very different. Rivers are found in nearly every part of the country holding barbel; in many of them barbel of ten, eleven, twelve and thirteen pounds are caught frequently. Some rivers produce 14- and even 15-pounders every season.

In certain stretches of the Ouse, whoppers as large as over twenty pounds have been taken, where even a 22-pounder is a realistic target for a very keen specialist to hope for. What a difference from the 1960s, when a 13-pounder was a dream come true and 14-pounders were all myths from the past!

Bob Church and I have been good mates for a very long time. He's an all-rounder – game, coarse and sea – and now (approaching three-score-and-ten), after many years at the top of trout fishing, he's back with the barbel.

He caught his first 10-pounder from the Royalty (Pipe Bridge Slack) in the 1960s, on a memorable day when we were fishing together. It is now the Ouse that holds his interest. He's already through the 14lb and 15lb barriers, and, who knows, a 20-pounder might just be waiting for his next cast....

But Bob is a realist, and knows that catching some big barbel from one stretch of one river is not enough to make him an all-embracing expert. And that is why, in this welcome book, he has gathered together a team of top barbel specialists to cover the methods, baits, rigs, tactics and much else of the modern scene.

Pete Reading, Ray Walton, Guy Robb and Brian Dowling are all men I know and respect as highly motivated, highly successful, dedicated barbel men; they know the game inside out.

My best barbel weighed 12lb 7oz – a significant achievement at the time – but now, armed with the wealth of information contained in this book, I know I can do better. You can too. Enjoy!

Peter Wheat
Poole, Dorset

5

Introduction

by Bob Church

You name it, I've done it, from all the main game fish, right through to all the coarse fish. A true all-rounder I like to fish for specimens, or big catches. 'I have more enthusiasm today than I did when I was younger, because I am a much better angler with age.' Barbel are a big love of mine at the moment. The river Ouse in particular is right close to home, but I have caught barbel from the Teme, Hampshire Avon, the Dorset Stour, the Trent, the Ure and some of those big Spanish river giants, such as the river Tormes at Salamanca.

I have made a lot of new friends through just barbel fishing these past four years, including the Northampton Specimen Group's barbel enthusiasts and Steve Curtin, the former barbel record-holder who is an incredibly good barbel fisher, and so modest. Then there is Adrian Busby, Nigel Collins, Graham King, Dick Bateman, Ray House, Trevor Wilson, Graham Attwood, Stuart Court, Mel Bellingham, Steve Grey, Paul Thompson, Mark Ward, Vince Rogers, Tony Gibson and the four co-authors of this book. Hence the book's title, *Big Barbel – Bonded by the Challenge*. This is my eleventh book, I do hope you enjoy it. If you don't already fish for barbel you soon will after reading this.

ABOUT THE AUTHORS
by Bob Church

Why did I pick these four anglers to contribute to my book? First and foremost, they can all catch their fair share of barbel. I also know that Ray, Guy and Pete are held in high esteem and have a lot to give with their specialized tactics. Its great to read just how they do it season after season. They certainly have caught an awful lot of barbel between them.

Were you thinking I had forgotten Brian Dowling? – no way. He may not be in the news so much for catching outsize barbel, as he tends to spend a lot of his time fishing in his local river, the Dove. Although a beautiful river, barbel don't grow as big there as they do in the Great Ouse, the Hampshire Avon and Stour, and so on. Nonetheless, he has caught his share of doubles, some fifty plus of them. Brian is the most dedicated record keeper I have ever met. His researched collection is a main attraction at all of the barbel specialist club conferences. His work, as you will read, just had to go down as an historical record for all barbel anglers now and in the future to study.

1 A Taste for Barbel

by Bob Church

I began my fishing for barbel back in the early 1960s. In those days I would spend a week's holiday, down south somewhere in Hampshire. Sooner or later I would then find myself sitting on the banks of the Hampshire Avon at the famous Royalty fishery. Or it could be a few miles down the road to Throop fishery on the Dorset Stour. Both these places drew me and my friend, the late Frank Wright, quite often in the years that followed.

At that time, barbel were a sort of up-market luxury big fish to try for. For my trips south I would sometimes meet up with top barbel men of their time, Peter Wheat and Dave Steuart. Peter would tend to build up a swim (that is, like the Pipe Slack) on the Royalty, continuously feeding lots of maggots and also ground bait, then during the evening the barbel would move in and feed. I remember well, you had to be packed up and away before dark or else the then bailiff, Ken Keynes, would be after you. I have to admit, those last fifteen minutes were always the best for big barbel on the Royalty; I bet they still are.

The heaviest barbel I saw caught at the Royalty was in fact from this same swim, but it was hooked in the centre of the river, in the deeper fast current. A London angler whom I knew only as Sam used to fish a large piece of bread flake on a size no. 2 hook. This he would cast into the fast centre channel flow holding bottom with a centrally threaded heavy coffin lead. His rod was 13ft split cane and he set the rod rest so the rod was high up. The bite detector was a centrepin reel on ratchet.

Halfway through my week's holiday in 1965, I had caught a few nice barbel and chub. I was fishing downstream of Sam but I looked up to see quite a few anglers watching him play a big fish. I soon arrived as well, in time to see him net a beautiful 13lb 4oz specimen barbel. It was a magnificent fish and I remember saying to myself, 'I'll catch one like that one day.' At the time this was an absolute monster.

BARBEL IN THE OUSE

The stocking of the river Severn with barbel in the early 1960s is one of the greatest gambles ever to pay off in modern-day fishery management. The fish have found the Severn very much to their liking and so the reproduction rate has been high.

Every angler who fishes the river has benefited from this. Match weights have been boosted considerably since the barbel began to show up in numbers, while specimen hunters and casual anglers have made impressive catches. In fact, everyone who visits the Severn these days is secretly after the barbel.

All this at the time left anglers in my locality asking 'Why can't we have some Barbel in the Great Ouse?' The Northampton Nene AC own much of the fishing rights from Olney downstream to Carlton. The question of stocking club waters at Newton Blossomville and Turvey was brought up by myself and Frank Wright at the annual meeting, when it was suggested that barbel would be most at home in these lengths. We were sure that barabel could breed easily giving good sport to both match men and specimen hunters. The AGM of the club agreed.

The meeting was in favour of pursuing the matter further, but after looking into it, they found that barbel stock was impossible to obtain. Eight years passed, then the situation changed. With roach still very short on the stretches mentioned and the bream only rarely co-operating, we were sure that the barbel would fill the gap handsomely.

Yes, we did know that barbel were already present in small numbers on some stretches of the Great Ouse, but in the main these came from well downstream of Bedford. During that period a few barbel had been caught at Hemmingford Grey, in a weir pool. My good friend Ian Howcroft of Luton discovered the spot, but it would be true to say that the fish are few and far between, even if their smallish size is proof of some successful breeding.

Many years earlier Dick Walker caught six fine barbel of between 6–9lb from Offord Weirpool but little has been heard since of such fish coming from that area.

It would be so nice, though, to have a barbel river on our doorstep and I thought this could be achieved if a fair stocking of fish were put in the right place. After looking at the Ouse over the years (almost from its source to where it enters the sea), I was confident that the gravelly shallows complete with streamer weed at Turvey and Newton Blossomville, would suit barbel so well that they would reproduce in much greater numbers. This would trigger off a more general stocking of the river as some

fish dropped downstream from time to time.

The stumbling block was where to get the barbel, and to get support from the river authority. Mind you, they had given us permission to stock eight years earlier, but we had failed to obtain any barbel at that time.

With the river Severn absolutely teeming with small barbel, I was sure an arrangement could be considered, whereby, say, 100 fish could be transferred to the Ouse. It would be a very small loss to the Severn, but could well be the making of great things to come for the Ouse! So it was that in the 1969–70 season, sixty barbel were given to the Northampton Nene club by Des Kelsall, the Severn River Board officer at the time.

These fish were put in at Lavendon, and weighed between 1½lb up to about 3lb. True to my theory these fish bred successfully at Turvey and Harrold and so have populated the river downstream to Bedford. So Frank and myself did our bit by nagging the committee and just look what we have now.

Barbel fishing is infectious and its numbers of one-species anglers is spreading rapidly today. The Barbel Society is a well organized association with 1,500 members. More recently, I helped form the Barbel Specialist Association, of which there are about sixty dedicated members. I reckon that barbel are now tying for second place with the pike for species popularity. Of course, the carp is still miles ahead of all of them put together.

For the last four years I have been taking a very active interest in the barbel again. One of the reasons for this is, that my local river the Great Ouse has continued to develop into the finest barbel river in the country. My keen trout fishing friend, John Emerson, and I had both decided to concentrate on barbel about the same time.

John Emerson with his 12lb 9oz barbel caught at Turvey, July 2001.

We approached it all quite effectively, and joined in the local open entry clubs that had good stretches on the Great Ouse – for example, Northampton Nene AC with waters we both knew well at Turvey, Lavendon, Newton Blossomville and Harrold. Then the Vauxhall Club with their waters at Radwell, Felmersham and Sharnbrook, the Milton Keynes Angling Association that has Ravenstone Mill, Gayhurst and the now club-syndicated stretch, Adams Mill. Finally, the Newport Pagnell Angling Club that has lots of the river Ouse in and around the little town, most of which holds big barbel and a healthy stock of them.

John and I found it quite difficult to begin with, as we retrod the footsteps where I fished for chub so many years ago. However, once we got a decent fish or two on the bank, things soon came together. John was doing particularly well with doubles at Turvey, and he eventually caught barbel up to 14lb there. At the same time this was a new best fish for the stretch (now up to 15lb 8oz).

I then spread my wings and joined the Milton Keynes club and went to look at the Adams Mill stretch, I had heard so much about. I went there for the first time in late June 1999. I was doing a bit of barbel spotting toward the downstream end of the fishery, when I saw it. A monster barbel, it had to be 16lb plus and I could see it quite distinctly in the crystal-clear shallow water. I got so excited I just knew I would be fishing that stretch in the future.

Later, about midday, I walked back upstream to the weir. There, Stef Horak and Peter Reading were fishing the maggot very effectively, and catching a few barbel. I sat back on the bank and we chatted. They gave me some good information as to what swims to fish and so on for the future.

Adams Mill was only twenty minutes' drive from my home, so I decided I wanted to give it a good go. On those early sessions I noticed two anglers were catching most of the big fish. Graham Attwood and Trevor Wilson, who came from North London, were indeed very successful. They had what they termed their special paste

9

The famous 'Bridge Swim' at Adams Mill.

bait, which was and probably still is, very very good. Trevor said to me: 'Bob get yourself a good sweet bait, "Boilie and paste" and then stick to it.'

This I did using my long-term favourite caramel-flavour base, and I got John Baker to make me 10kg of it. However, it was a maggot feeder that gave me my first two Adams Mill barbel hook-ups. I have been catching as many as eight barbel in a session (up to 8lb) lower down the river, but I hooked my first Adams fish after fifteen sessions. I was fishing in the Bend swim. I was using 8lb nylon and got snapped off in the barbel's first short and powerful fast run. The feeder scraped along the bottom with the powerful speed of the fish and ping! Needless to say I was pig sick. I did confide in Phil Smith who was fishing in the 'Straight' near by. One week later, Phil phoned me to ask if I wanted my hook back, he said 'I'll keep the swivel for luck'. 'Phil, the weight, what was the weight?' I

pleaded. 'Only 14lb' he laughed. I did feel a bit of a twit really.

Now, into January and toward the end of the month, I had another take in the same swim with the same feeder maggot rig, the only difference being this time that I had 12lb nylon on, with similar in fluoro-carbon for my hook link. I was very, very pleased to land a new PB at 12lb 12oz – a beauty. This was much admired as the water temperatures were down to 40.5°F. I was on my way but it had taken about twenty sessions. Some good barbel had come out as the season drew to an end in March 2000. John Barford had been prominent with a few good doubles that had gone up to 16lb 15oz. Then Warren Day had five doubles in a day while fishing the 'Straight'. They weighed 12lb 6oz, 12lb 10oz, 12lb 14oz, 12lb 15oz and 13lb 15oz. Later, on another trip, he had a fish of 16lb 14oz.

Then the name of Guy Robb kept cropping up and he and Stuart Morgan started

Adams Mill upstream of the bridge in high summer.

Guy Robb holds 15lb of 'Teardrop' caught in 'The Straight', Adams Mill, early July 2001.

to do the business about a mile downstream at the 'Kickles'. Guy broke the record with a 17lb 6oz 12dr fish, but with just a couple of days left to the season, Trevor Wilson landed the fish known as 'Red Belly' in the 'Straight' swim. Due to a technicality after the fish got snagged and Trevor changed banks, the record claim was dropped. His friend Graham had passed the rod over to him so he could free the snag. At 17lb 10oz it was, in the opinion of the fair-minded, a new record. Everyone could see that the barbel in general were packing on weight rapidly in the two plus mile-stretch of the Great Ouse from Adams weir to Newport Pagnell weir.

In July 2000, I started to catch a few from Adams and the Baker/Church caramel boilies were working. My best fish went 14lb 4oz from the top 'Hole' caught at midday in blazing sunshine. Funny, but between noon and 2pm turned out to be a really good time for a take at Adams, and still is. Ask Paul Thompson, as in the latter part of the 2004 season he had three personal-best barbel from the Mill going at 14lb 3oz, 14lb 4oz and 14lb 14oz – such success after years of concentrating hard during the period from dawn till 10am, and then again the last two hours up to darkness. (Remember no night fishing is allowed at Adams.) I nearly forgot – Paul did use the new stone weights for the first time when catching these three barbel.

Some of the larger barbel along the Adams to Kickles stretch now have names.

Guy Robb with 'The Traveller, 18lb 10oz, caught at the 'Kickles'.

Bob holding a 14lb 4oz beauty caught at noon on an August Bank Holiday Monday at Adams Mill.

Paul Thompson with a personal-best fish weighing 14lb 14oz caught at 'Lower Bridge', in flood using a Stoneze Ledger.

Dick Bateman lands another of Paul Thompson's barbel, this one weighing 14lb 4oz.

The two largest were definitely 'The Pope' and 'Red Belly'. Others close behind were 'Stumpy', 'the Traveller', 'Teardrop', 'Gregory Peck', 'Liner' and 'Broken Back'. Some of the Adams and Kickles regulars were now co-operating with each other on growth rates and identification through photographs, and so on.

The biggest eye-opener for myself, Paul Thompson, Gareth Hancock and Tony Gibson, came during the season 2000 and just into January 2001, when soon after, all fishing was stopped because of the very bad foot-and-mouth epidemic.

Paul had netted the fish known as the 'Pope' for his friend Steve Frapwell on 24 June 2000. It was hooked on float-fished trotted worm and weighed 15lb 4oz. It was now Saturday, 2 September and I had got up early to fish the Adams stretch. I could not believe it was 6am and no-one else was around. At 9am I was still the only one there. I had chosen to fish the 'Snag swim' as I had spotted a few barbel in and around it.

I decided to phone Gareth Hancock, who was still in bed following a night's clubbing in town. He was a bit hung over but I insisted that he get in the shower and come over to Adams, to get his choice of swims. He did just that but arrived about 9.30am. As well as arriving late for the fishing, Gareth also appeared without a proper landing net and with only a small amount of bait. That meant he had to borrow (as he termed it), some bait and bits from me. Gareth had in fact broken his big landing net handle on his last trip and had not replaced it – also he had only a small amount of paste bait.

He had tied up some hair-rigs but the link from the hook to the stopper was too long. So we threaded on two of my caramel boilies to cater for the long link. Gareth settled in the swim just downstream of me and began fishing. About an hour later, I hooked an 11-pounder and whistled to Gareth to come and take a picture for me. As Gareth went back to his swim he decided to cross the shallow gravel cattle drink below it and look into his swim from the high bank on the other side. It was then that he nearly had a heart attack. There were no less than eleven barbel in his swim. He threw in some pellets upstream and as they came down with the current and reached the bottom, the barbel began to feed.

Of course, he couldn't get back to his swim quick enough. The bite came at 1.45pm and he was into a big fish. It was at this stage that Gareth realized his temporary landing net was not big enough. Panic set in when his efforts to alert me failed; as I was upwind his shouts never reached me.

So Gareth is now playing a potential record fish with his right hand and phoning me on the mobile with his left. I soon arrived to net this huge, deep barbel safely, and as I did so a third angler arrived, Tony from London.

I confidently said, 'a new British record, Gareth', and all three witnessed the correct weighing at 17lb 7oz on a new set of Reubon Heaton scales. The fish, in fact, was 'The Pope' and it had put on 2lb 1½oz of weight since 24 June, when it was last caught. A weights and measures check of the scales said they were weighing 1½oz heavy when between 14½lb and 18lb so that put it at 17lb 5½oz. Certainly the largest summer barbel ever caught and an ounce below Guy's record at the time.

Then on 4 January, our good friend and Northampton Specimen Group member, Tony Gibson was night fishing at Kickles Farm half a mile downstream of Adams. It was full-flood conditions when the 'Pope' came to the bait again to a paste that Tony had specially made up. This time he weighed in at 19lb 1oz, which of course, was a new record. Stuart Morgan's two 17lb plus fish had not had time to be ratified – but this was a remarkable situation of how barbel can put on weight in the river Great Ouse. It had achieved 4lb 2oz of body weight since 16 June. The same fish has not been caught for coming up to

Gareth Hancock proudly holds 'The Pope' that he caught at Adams Mill in September 1999 when the fish weighed 17lb 5½ oz.

*Gareth Hancock
returns 'The Pope'.*

three years now and Adrian Busby was probably the last to bank it. We all saw the 'Pope' at great size in the summer of 2003, where it lay downstream of the bridge at Adams. The water was gin-clear and many barbel took refuge under the bridge in the low, clear water. We all estimated the fish to be over 20lb; for proof, the 'Traveller' was also there and came out at 19lb 2oz but he looked a bit smaller than the 'Pope'.

My opinion of Steve Curtin's ability to catch large barbel could not be higher. I think Ray Walton is also of this opinion. Steve has caught every one of the largest named fish, not once but twice. In 2003, he then moved many miles downriver to Radwell where he again caught the largest barbel outside the Adams/Kickles stretch whose weight was 16lb 2oz. Vince Rogers is in a similar bracket but he doesn't catch lots of fish at Adams and district. I believe, in the 2003 season, he caught six of the big ones, five were barbel, and these were topped by a 7lb chub. So you see one way

and another I am surrounded by very cool barbel anglers.

Apart from my Belly Buster semi-soft boilies of caramel and salmon oils, I was able to catch quite well on one of the other simple boilie baits. This is excellent in summer months. It is pellets and pellet dust mixed with eggs, a little olive oil and some clear gelatine.

Chopping and changing with different baits seldom works. The successful, consistent regulars find a good bait and stick to it. Just look at ex-record holder Steve Curtin's catches – he swears by this simple rule. Various boilies, pastes and pellets are favourites at the moment, but the 'Stef method' with plenty of maggots or casters can still be the best of all, especially if the water is low and clear enough to see the barbel.

Some very good anglers have come to fish this famous stretch of the Ouse and always leave respecting it. As I found out, once you crack it, you can get on a bit of a

Graham King with 'Broken Back', weighing over 15lb, captured at 'Top Hole', Adams Mill, in late September 2003.

roll. Quite amazingly, out of my first twelve double-figure barbel catches, only one was a repeat capture, even though the same swims were being fished.

Apart from the three very big fish that turn up two or three times each season, the back-up doubles are getting heavier as well. For example, my first five autumn fish in 2002 in eleven daytime trips, weighed 13lb, 13lb 6oz, 13lb 8oz, 14lb 2oz and 14lb 8oz with a 5lb 4oz chub for good measure. Now I know that five fish from eleven days' fishing is not many, but each barbel would have been the fish of a lifetime up to two or three seasons back, and probably still is.

For the four seasons, Paul Thompson and I have carried out an identification study of any 12lb-plus barbel caught from Adams Mill. I have kept a scrapbook that is now full of every press picture and privately obtained colour photo. With the help of a powerful magnifying glass, it is easy to identify the same fish that are caught at different weights as the season progresses. Obviously, after spawning in late June they are at their lightest and as the season approaches on 14 March, they are at their heaviest. Now that Steve Curtin, Ray Walton, Stuart Court and others have taken an interest, we all hope to learn far more about this unique stretch in the future.

The 'Pope' always had a swimming mate when I first fished the Mill – the now dead barbel known as 'Red Belly', which was always a little lighter in weight. It came out

The 'beauty spots' that are useful identification marks, and that are a characteristic of many barbel at the 'Mill Stretch', can clearly be seen in this picture of a fish that weighed in at 15lb 12 oz. It is known as 'Liner'.

Vince Rogers with a magnificent 18lb 11oz fish named 'The Traveller' that he caught at Adams Mill in September 2003.

in the summer of 2001 at 17lb 2oz and again in early September at 17lb 15oz. By late October it had rocketed in weight to 19lb 6½oz and became the new national record capture for Steve Curtin. It did show again, twice more from different swims, at 18lb 13½oz to Ray Walton and 18lb 13oz to Vince Rogers.

Why are the barbel so big above Newport Pagnell? We have all been theorizing on this one for a few years. Certainly there are less fish here than lower

A beautiful 15lb 9oz specimen caught at 'Hollow Tree', Adams Mill, by Nigel Collins.

downstream. Therefore there is less competition for natural food. Add to this the amount of high protein bait that gets thrown in and you have part of the answer. There must be other reasons though.

Ray Walton finished the season of 2002 in great style, taking ten fish in the final three weeks. He really is the master of the 'rolled meat', warm flood, centrepin reel method. Steve Curtin and I managed two respectable doubles at 15lb 11oz for Steve and 15lb 2oz for me. Yes, our boilies and paste came back on form as the temperature began to rise.

In general I look on the current barbel fishing on the Great Ouse as exciting and challenging, as good as any I have faced in over fifty years of serious specimen hunting. No angler could fail to be completely 'gob smacked' once they have seen a 17lb plus fish on the bank. So far, the closest I have been is when netting the 'Pope' for Gareth Hancock. But ambitions are there to be fulfilled. Meanwhile I will keep up

the campaign and will not moan if I can keep this average size up.

I suppose Adams Mill has probably become the best known stretch of river anywhere in the country. I admit to being completely absorbed by the place and can enjoy myself just walking, talking and socializing, and very importantly, fish spotting. In the latter case, I mean more than just finding fish – I mean studying the fish's behaviour.

In the last week of September in very low gin-clear water, there was only Paul Thompson and myself at the Mill. Beneath the bridge, in clear view, we watched a number of fish for a long time. There was a British record barbel and another that was almost as big. A solitary huge roach, well over 4lb, was also present. In addition I could see five chub over 5lb with one of them being a monster of about 7½lb, and finally a perch of about 3½lb. Most anglers who have visited the fishery during that period have seen these fish.

Ron Randall with his personal best barbel of 15lb 12oz, called 'Liner', that he caught on the Great Ouse.

Mark Ward with a fine fish weighing 13lb 7oz that he caught at 'Two Trees Swim', Adams Mill, on 16 June 2001.

Paul started to fish under the bridge while I watched their reactions with just my head sticking out it. He fished as light as he dared and used lobworm rather than the usual boilie. The bait sometimes dropped within a couple of feet of the roach, but it never even looked at it. The two monster barbel would drop back downstream a few yards before moving slowly forward close to the lobworm where they simply looked at it. Even the big perch was having none of it and the chub appeared totally oblivious to everything!

Paul did eventually catch five perch, with the best close to 2lb. I watched this for around two hours and it was completely fascinating.

Mark Ward has built up something of a reputation for catching the first Adams barbel of the season – and he did it again in June 2002 with an excellent 13lb 7oz fish from the 'Two Trees' swim. This turned into a double PB when he caught a 6lb 4oz chub later in the morning.

I also had a decent chub that opening day, landing a 5lb 3oz fish – and later I caught further fish of 5lb 12oz, 5lb 9oz, 5lb 7oz and 5lb 5oz, plus several over 4lb. Quite a few other members have targeted a massive chub that we all see regularly, but cannot catch.

There was a period in July when Adams was invaded by large pike that probably came up from the deeper water downstream. Unfortunately, they had an appetite for big chub that shocked and surprised us. I did catch a long 17½lb pike from the 'Snag swim' and then moved him upstream above the weir. We caught several chub that had clearly been the victims of an attack.

It would seem that the shallow waters of Adams attract the chub, barbel, various small fish and, of course, the pike in the summer months. Although they move about from swim to swim quite a lot, they stay in the vicinity until around mid-November. Then most but not all drop back to the deeper, slower water downstream where the Ouse backwater stream rejoins the river.

This takes in the Newport Pagnell AC new syndicate stretch, plus Kickles and a whole stretch of unexplored deeper water at Lathbury, known for its good winter chub of over 7lb. The most spectacular incident so far was when Tim observed a 15lb pike taking a 5lb 10oz chub. Tim was barbel fishing a deep pool at the end of a shallow run as evening approached. The

Stuart Court with 'The Traveller' weighing 19lb 2oz that was captured at Adams Mill and proved to be the heaviest barbel of the 2003 season.

Fishing in winter flood conditions – first find the river! Then set the rod rests up high and take care while waiting for a bite.

Adams Mill, upstream of the bridge, in late-autumn flood conditions.

Bob Church takes advantage of the cover and finds a comfortable seat consisting of flood debris lodged in a tree.

Bob with an 8¼-pounder, his reward for fishing the winter flood.

water was gin-clear when suddenly he was aware of a violent struggle as the pike took the chub across its jaws and shook it, releasing a scattering of scales the size of 50p pieces.

I was fishing upstream at the time. Ray House had arrived at Tim's swim and, as I always carry a wire trace, swivel and lures at Adams these days, he came up to me to borrow a spinner. All was quiet by the time he got back to Tim's pool, but Ray cast out the spinner anyway. By sheer luck he foul-hooked the pike and soon had it in the net. What we saw was a bit of a nightmare – a massive tail was sticking out of the pike's mouth.

We were all at Tim's swim by now. We tried as carefully as possible to release the chub that was just about alive but lacerated and very badly descaled. We weighed it accurately at 5lb 10oz. Sadly the chub died but the pike had to find new living quarters as we put him back above the weir.

Graham King is a top carp man and a well-travelled angler, having caught big sailfish, wahoo and tarpon on the fly. Despite this, he began his Adams Mill barbel career with twenty-eight blanks. Nevertheless, he was determined to succeed and to his credit began to get a fish or two most times he fished. This all came to an amazing conclusion in a catch he made on 11

Bob returns a splendid 13lb 6oz fish.

July 2002, when he landed six double figure barbel. The river had risen about a foot or more and was dropping back to normal. Conditions were good and the catch came from four different swims. The fish weighed 14½lb, 14lb 1oz, 13½lb, 13lb 2oz, 12lb 4oz and 11½lb. This day-time catch weighed a total of 78lb 15oz and must be some sort of national record. (*See* Chapter 5.)

In fact, that's enough from me, let's see how the four experts catch their barbel. Finally, apologies for going on a bit about the Great Ouse. But you must admit, it's a pretty exciting river to be fishing for barbel just now.

Bob's grandson, Jordan Church, with a 13¼lb fish caught by grandad. Will Jordan become a barbel angler? Only time will tell.

Bob Church holds the 14lb 8oz barbel he caught on the Great Ouse in October 2003.

Pete Reading

Pete has fished for barbel ever since his appetite for the species was whetted on the famous Throop fishery in the 1960s. Although the barbel is his favourite species, he has fished with interest, and some success, for pike, tench, chub, roach and grayling, and maintains an impressive record of specimens for these species. Pete also regularly fishes the Avon, Dorset Stour and Frome for salmon and trout. He has caught double-figure barbel from the Avon, Stour, Great Ouse, Kennet and Severn, and seeks to fish more on the Bristol Avon and Teme, where he has caught plenty of fish but as yet no doubles!

He aims to use a wide range of approaches to barbel fishing, preferring to seek out and explore for new fish in new swims, and catch nearly all his fish in daylight hours. Pete is not a fan of night fishing or the troubles it can bring to both the fish and the fisheries.

Pete has fished for the biggest specimens available, but maintains a balanced view of fishing, and is just as happy to spend a day hunting a few shoal fish in a new swim on the Avon as he is sitting it out for well-known monsters on fisheries that hold record-breakers.

Over the years Pete has contributed numerous articles to the weekly and monthly angling press and to several books. He has been treasurer, fishery manager and latterly chairman of the biggest club in the south, the Christchurch Angling Club, and has assisted as regional organizer for NASA in the 1980s. He was a Barbel Society founder member and is currently acting as Research and Conservation officer for the Society. Pete held the barbel record unofficially, and briefly, with a 14-pounder from the Stour in the 1980s when the record was open at 13lb 12oz, although NASA still recognized the ancient 14lb 6oz records from the Royalty.

Pete is a staunch supporter of the Close Season on rivers as well as stillwaters.

Pete with the 13lb fish he caught on paste in early autumn on the Dorset Stour.

2 A Barbel Fisher's Year

by Pete Reading

Early season can be as difficult a time for the fisherman as it is for the fish. Those lovely June days can be so long, warm and pleasant that the catching of barbel can become secondary to the sheer joy of being out once again on the river bank after the painful, but so necessary, Close Season break.

The fresh green and often overgrown banks are part of an annual exploration of pastures new, even when the stretch is a familiar one, and the barbel are invariably as unsettled and unsure as we are about what they should be doing at the start of a new season.

Spawning is usually out of the way, but has often meant an urgent, hormone-driven migration from feeding areas to spawning beds of gravel or other suitable substrate that has scattered the fish from their usual haunts.

The shallow streamy water below weirs can be a likely spot to seek out fish, but they may be present in a swim for perhaps only a few hours before moving on and settling down to do some proper feeding, instead of courting and copulating.

Since my early-season barbel fishing is based around evening sessions after work, the roving approach with short stays in a

The barbel's nose. Who says they cannot smell?

series of likely looking spots is my most common style of fishing.

There is never any need to hurry, no urgent need to catch on the first day, and many is the time that 16 June has been a barbel blank for me, especially on the Avon or Stour, where barbel populations are relatively small and location is invariably hindered by coloured water due to early-season algal or diatom blooms. There should be no rush to catch barbel at that time of year, and trying too hard runs the risk of really spoiling the fun of it all.

I much prefer to take a nice relaxing start to the year, and not to have too high a level of expectation. Working out where the fish are likely to be, setting up your little ambush and savouring the anticipation of that first bite of the season is a key part of the enjoyment of fishing.

LATE JUNE ON THE STOUR

This year, the river was in perfect condition for once, after a heavy downpour in late May had flushed and cooled a Dorset Stour that is normally low, warm and tinged with reddish brown diatoms at this time of the season.

I had baited two or three swims with some new boilies that John Baker had

Pete Reading holds a beautiful 14lb 9oz specimen taken on the Dorset Stour on a small piece of boilie over a bed of pellets and crumbled boilies.

asked me to test out, and after some success in the last weeks of the previous season, I was eager to see if they were going to be good summer baits too. Baiting swims simply meant that I had fished them once or twice on previous occasions, and the actual process of fishing involved the introduction of perhaps twenty or thirty baits. Chub had shown an immediate interest, and no doubt had polished off most of my baits within minutes of me leaving the swims, when a further handful had been introduced.

At the time I was only starting to gain confidence in boilies and pastes, and the efficacy of smelly paste in floodwater had been demonstrated to me in no uncertain terms the previous autumn and winter.

This stretch is nice and easy to get to, no long walks involved and handy safe parking. No time to lose when perhaps there were only a few hours of fishing available before dark.

I had fished this swim on two occasions earlier in the week, with only a few small chub to show for it. I was encouraged to hear that another angler had taken an 11-pounder just downstream, but it was the usual slow start to the season it seemed, with no other fish reported on the stretch to date. Maybe the fish were upstream, just below the weir where I had seen them spawning as early as April in previous years, maybe they were downstream, on the gravelly shallows above the next weir down, maybe they were in the swim round the bend, just above Alf's Hole, where someone had reported seeing a shoal of barbel dashing about on the shallows, apparently ignoring all attempts to catch them. Maybe I should be tench fishing!

All these thoughts were milling around in my head as I deposited a 2oz lead and delectable boilie wrapped in delicious paste into the middle of the river where I

A 12-pounder caught on boilies in bright sunlight at Throop on the Dorset Stour.

remembered there was a nice clear, clean depression in the gravel.

There was thick weed just upstream and also below the swim, and I had made some exploratory casts to ensure that I was fishing on open gravel. The water was still too coloured to see into, and the recent flood ensured that there was plenty of drifting silkweed and other debris to make holding station quite difficult. A 1oz drilled bullet was employed as a flying backlead, held in place about six feet from the main lead by a rubber float stop. The backlead meant that I could hold out in what was quite a substantial flow, while others were struggling to fish at all, complaining about kids swimming upstream or weirgates being opened as the cause for all the debris.

Even local anglers on the Avon and Stour will fail to fish with a heavy enough

29

lead to hold bottom properly when bar-belling, and I will commonly employ 3oz or even 4oz, even in normal flows to ensure that the bait is nailed down.

I also make sure that the rod tip is kept low, often below the water surface, to keep the line out of the way of drifting weed, a common curse on the southern rivers. So often you see people with rods pointing skyward, in the misplaced belief that the lead holds better or that they can see the bites more easily, perhaps? In fact, as a general rule, such a set-up holds less well than with the rod tip underwater, and only results in catching more weed than fish. Although there is less line in the water,

what line there is, is in the faster surface current, and the lead is soon shifted by either the pressure of flow on the line, or drifting debris.

My rod was snuggled down in the nettles, with the tip just under the surface, and I was able to keep a bait out for an hour or more while others were struggling to hold for more than a few minutes.

Time passed in the hot evening sunshine, and the occasional knock from a little chub was all that the irresistible Baker bait seemed likely to produce. I flicked in the odd boilie or lump of paste, and was encouraged by the way that the hordes of marginal minnows attacked the bait that I

A 12-pounder caught in the Dorset Stour in June. This fish went on to weigh just over 15lb at the end of the season.

This 13-pounder from the Dorset Stour was taken on paste in early autumn.

dropped in the edge. I was sure that they were doing the same to the paste wrapped around the boilie out in the barbel swim, but was confident that the underlying hard bait would resist their attentions for some time.

I had also baitdropped some crumbled boilie at the start of the session, a difficult tactic to resist when I was so used to particle fishing for barbel with hemp or pellet in conjunction with maggot, caster or corn. I was wondering, should I really have made the decision to leave out hemp altogether when fishing these baits, when the rod hammered round in announcement of my first barbel of the season.

The centrepin screeched as I dived to pick up the rod that was now being dragged through the nettles, and I was relieved and elated to feel once again the awesome power of what was undoubtedly a barbel of good size. It cruised irresistibly across the river, turned and burrowed up into the streamer weed, and stopped. Good, thought I, he won't go any further. As so often happens, he read my thoughts and decided to make another unstoppable run into the weed, by now burying himself in what seemed like ten yards of thick, young, strong streamer weed. The weed on this stretch of the Stour is really tough, and brute strength is no way to deal with it. I was grateful for the confidence I had in the brand of robust 12lb line I was employing, and it has to be said that boilie fishing with heavy leads does need line of high breaking strain and durability. Hard-fighting barbel of high average size do demand sensible gear.

When barbel become snagged like this, the only way to rescue them is to patiently wait until they kick themselves out, so I did just that. Whenever the fish gave a kick, I pulled back gently, and eventually gained the initiative; a big fat barbel was soon thumping about under the rod top. The tail that was waving disdainfully at me a few times before it finally tired was an indication of its size, and soon almost 12½lb of solid bronze Stour barbel was gasping in the net. I recognized the fish immediately as one that I had taken the previous season at a weight of almost 15lb, which shows just how much weight they can gain throughout the year and then lose, presumably, in the rigours of spawning.

It is common for a summer 12-pounder to put on 2lb or more as the season pro-gresses, although fish can sometimes still be very heavy in the early season if they fail to lose all their spawn, or spawn really early and then pig out in their post-coital feeding spell.

Such a fish would be enough to set any-one up for the season, but I was fortunate enough to take another 12-pounder that evening, and two more doubles the follow-ing evening from the same swim. An 8-pounder that fought harder than any of the doubles rounded it off, so what a fantastic first week to the season. The bait had proved itself, and I had deliberately fished it without any hemp attractor, just to prove

A hump-backed winter barbel in prime condition, weighing 14lb 10oz. This fish was taken from a flooded Dorset Stour using a John Baker paste.

This lean, hungry and well-coloured Hampshire Avon 13-pounder was caught in June on a JB boilie after 'pre-baiting'.

that it is not always necessary. It was difficult after so many years of hemping, but it had to be done to prove to myself that the bait itself had the inherent attractiveness that I had been assured it did.

I still do not fish with boilies and paste as exclusively as some, but I now have that extra technique in the armoury that will catch fish that might otherwise not have come my way. It is also good to do something different!

JULY ON THE AVON

By the time mid-July comes round, the Avon has often lost the early-season tinge, the ranunculus is up and growing strongly, and it is possible to search out and spot fish, which is really the essence of Hampshire Avon barbel fishing.

Compared to some smaller rivers, the barbel population of the middle Avon is quite small, with good lengths of river devoid of fish. The barbel shoals are highly localized and groups of fish can be hard to track down. They can also be fairly mobile being there one day and gone the next. Location is crucial, therefore, and it is always worth spending a lot of time spotting, walking the correct bank at the correct time of day, armed with a rod, baitdropper and bucket of hemp. The river runs roughly from north to south, so the east bank is best inspected in the morning, and the west bank in the afternoon, so that the sun is at your back as much as possible. It is difficult to see in from the low, flat banks, and spotting trees are a rarity in the flat green floodplain.

Patience and persistence is needed too, and it is often necessary to stand stock still,

33

Mechanical weed-cutting destroying barbel habitat on the Hampshire Avon.

scouring a swim for signs of fish for several minutes at a time. It can be easy to give up, and wander off in search of the frustratingly elusive Avon barbel, when a few more minutes of scanning would have picked out the flick of a fin or gentle flashing of a flank under a weedbed.

Sometimes a few droppers of bait in a likely looking swim can bring fish, that would otherwise be invisible, from out of the weed or from under the bank. Sometimes you just have to fish a swim because it looks good, and the sixth sense of barbel detection can come into play. Sometimes, of course, the barbel will be sunning themselves in the open, and almost daring you to fish for them. These are the sort of barbel that so often melt away and disappear, never to be seen again, however, this engaging unpredictability is part of their attraction, and what can make

Avon barbel fishing so challenging and rewarding.

Fishing with caster and hemp is a deadly method for Avon barbel in the early summer, and if you are the first to come across a shoal you can clean up, accounting for most of the fish on the first day, picking up any stragglers if you are able to fish the swim two days running. Bright, hot conditions are ideal for this sort of fishing, and a nice long, relaxing day interspersed with the excitement of playing a few good fish is my idea of proper barbel fishing.

There is a stretch upstream of Ringwood that is one of the prettiest and most enigmatic bits of river I know. I well remember taking Martin Bowler for his first day on the river after the barbel. Martin was dead keen to catch a barbel from the Avon, and we elected to fish quite close together at Ellingham, just upstream of the bridge. We

A nicely coloured 12-pounder from the Hampshire Avon.

strolled about in the early part of the day, and soon found a couple of swims that I knew had some form, and where I had noticed one or two fish a few days earlier. We were each armed with three pints of caster and about six of hemp, which is generally enough for a good long day's fishing, and the routine was soon outlined to Martin.

As a general rule, once you have decided where to fish within the swim, put in ten or twelve droppers of hemp and caster in a 50/50 mix and leave it for at least half an hour before casting in. Go for a walk, have a cup of tea and a chat, but do not start fishing too soon, even if the fish are responding very positively to the initial baiting. Quite often it pays to give them a second dose of bait, and go off for another stroll, and if you can control yourself, and resist that temptation to cast in amongst feeding fish that seem to be begging to be

caught, you will probably be lucky enough to catch most of them.

If you cast in too early, on the other hand, before they have had time to gain confidence and to settle down to some determined feeding, imprinting themselves into the swim, you may get a fish first cast but no more for the rest of the day. When fish are a bit nervous or spooky, it may be necessary to feed them carefully for hours before a cast with a baited hook is made. This is where careful study of their behaviour and reactions is essential, but it is also useful to remember in swims where you cannot see the fish. Martin and I could see the fish quite clearly, however, and it was not long before he had his first Avon barbel, fishing a tricky far bank swim under an overhanging bush. Martin was soon to catch a load more fish from the river, including a terrific bag that included five double-figure fish, but on this occasion he

The weeds and reeds of the Hampshire Avon in summer at Bisterne.

was more than pleased with an 8-pounder for his inaugural barbel.

The fish in my swim were really numerous and hungry, and as is often the case, the biggest fish were the first to come out, including a fine brace of 9lb 11oz and 12lb 2oz in the first two casts. When they are going well on the casters they can seem almost suicidal, and by mid-afternoon I think that nine fish had fallen to my rod.

I had baited up under the rod top, leaving the swim for well over an hour before casting in, and these barbel were certainly being very obliging. The fish were holed up under a thick, far bank weedbed, but were drawn out over some open gravel to a nice little hole under a fan of streamer beneath

my feet. I saw several tails waving about from behind the weed before I thought they were confident enough to be fished for. They had not been fished much, however, and in subsequent visits they became a good deal cagier. One particularly big fish I spotted evaded me altogether, but I think came out later in the season as a big 13-pounder.

Although not strictly necessary in a close-in swim, I usually fish the casters in conjunction with a large heavy block-feeder, not so much to attract the fish to the hook-bait as to help with casting. It is much easier to be accurate with a big feeder, by overcasting and then allowing it to drop into place, than it is to cast a bomb directly into the swim. It is also less scary for the fish, especially when they are a bit edgy.

BISTERNE REVISITED

Although I think that the numbers of barbel on the Avon have declined in recent years, it is still possible to accumulate a bag of nine or ten fish in a day on most stretches, and the number of doubles and the average size are both increasing. A day on the river in summer is quite satisfactory if you get four or five fish, however, and most shoals contain a double or two these days. It is not uncommon to get two doubles in a day, which was almost unheard of in the 1970s and 1980s.

This year, in the company of my old friend John Found, I managed three in a day, which is something I have only achieved once before on the Avon. John was in typical relaxed mood, and seemed quite happy just to sit and chat and watch the fishing. He is no stranger to the southern rivers, but was interested to see how I tackled the fishing on a new stretch that he had not fished before, and where, I, myself had only tried once before, nearly twenty years previously.

As we made our preliminary inspection, we soon found a shoal of fish sitting out in the open in some very fast and shallow water. We pondered for a while on how best to approach them, and after leaving them with a few droppers of hemp deposited in the only available patch of weed, we wandered further upstream to an area that seemed deeper, and a little more weedy. We saw no barbel, but it smelled of them to me. The only real cover was some overhanging trees on the far bank, and a long thin bed of streamer in the middle of the river, but there was something about the swim that got my barbel senses twitching. I

put some more bait in just this side of the streamer, and we returned to the first swim. The barbel were very spooky, and had obviously been fished for so it would not be easy to get them feeding with any confidence.

We continued our investigation of the fishery, noting one or two nice features well downstream, and generally having a bit of a reminisce. I remembered fishing here many years ago, and catching a couple of 9-pounders which were very big fish in those days. An 11-pounder taken by a lady angler had featured in the angling press at the time, and was mentioned in hushed tones by the barbel fishing fraternity of that era. I had looked into the swim she had supposedly caught it from, and wondered if I would ever catch a fish so huge.

An 11-pounder was a real event in those days, and John and I spent some time discussing how things had changed, not only on the Avon, but nationally, with regard to the average size of barbel. A double-figure fish was your target for the whole season, and I can still hear myself saying that I would achieve a lifetime ambition by catching a 12-pounder from the Avon. Thirteen-pounders were the stuff of history or unattainable dreams, and the 14-pounders that held the record for decades were so unimaginable as to be seriously doubted by some. Fish of such size could not possibly have existed, surely those old boys had weighed them wrongly, it was said. How things can change. With a lower population, a bit of global warming, and possibly a bit more angler's bait, the size of barbel, as with most species, is on an upward trend that shows little sign of slowing down. It will do eventually, of course, but let us make the most of it for now!

Back to the swim that smelled of barbel to me, and we were greeted by the sight of what appeared to be four double-figure barbel grubbing about on my baited patch.

One of them looked to be substantially bigger than the rest, with great paddle-like fins and a depth and length that had us both guessing wildly at its weight. The sight of these lovely big barbel, with chocolate brown backs, brassy flanks and coral red fins confirmed for me what must be a large part of the attraction of Avon barbelling. To see such fish drifting about in the dappled sunlight in that swim is still in my mind's eye now.

John has a mature and unhurried approach to his fishing, and was happy just to sit and watch and see how those fish responded to being fished for. He settled down beside me, fed me tea and sandwiches, and watched me almost make a mess of it. I gave them another few droppers of hemp and caster mix, then tackled up as unhurriedly as I could. Despite my confident advice to John about leaving them to settle, to use the bait and then wait and wait a bit more, I cast in too quickly, ignoring my own advice! I soon realized my mistake, because the fish made a hasty departure, and became very nervous-looking.

I shared my concern with John, and was determined to retrieve the situation. While the fish were out of the swim, I put in more bait, this time almost a pint of neat caster, and promised myself and John not to cast in for an hour. It worked, and the fish eventually switched on, falling one by one to a bunch of five superglued hair-rigged casters on a long tail, once again nailed behind a heavy blockfeeder.

It was a difficult long cast to the feeding area, and the feeder had to be cast well beyond the baited spot, skimmed along the surface until it was in exactly the right spot, then dropped into position. This technique also ensured that the long hooklength straightened out and fell gently into place below the feeder. With plenty of open water and a hidey-hole under the far bank to try and get back to, those barbel fought like tigers, and every second of the struggle could be witnessed in the crystal-clear Avon water. They gave rod-wrenching bites, and tore off across the river with that strength and authority that I can never quite get used to. They thumped and bored

A blind 9-pounder from the Hampshire Avon; the fish had no eyeball at all.

An 11-pounder from the Hampshire Avon. This short, fat, healthy fish was taken from Bisterne on casters over hemp.

every inch of the way back to the net, always in view and a delight to watch.

The biggest-looking fish turned out to be a long, lean old soldier, which would have been well over 13lb in its prime, but was now probably in slow decline. The others were short, solid, stocky fish with plenty of growth left in them, and absolute pictures of health. Three were doubles, a big 10-pounder and two 11-pounders, and the fourth was a long but nice-looking 9-pounder, with one eye. Barbel that are apparently blind in one or both eyes are not uncommon, and they seem to cope with this infirmity admirably, usually being in good condition. They have senses for feeding and survival beyond the simply visual, and the blindness is probably caused by parasites of some sort.

The caster and hemp combination is now a firm favourite with me when considering a full day's fishing on the southern rivers. Three pints of caster and six of hemp is usually enough, and I now often take some 4mm trout pellet as an added attractor. On a hectic day, when the chub and barbel are particularly greedy, or when a change of swim has proved necessary, the couple of bags of pellet that are always in my luggage somewhere have often saved my bacon baitwise. It does not pay to run out of bait when particle fishing, so I always aim to carry more than enough, with some reserves in the car.

Caster will last a couple of days or more if kept sealed and cool, and are easy to carry the long distances to those more out-of-the way barbel swims. Casters are also ideal for supergluing on to a hair, and four or five stuck together on the tag of line from a knotless knot will stand up to a lot of abuse from small fish, yet remain attractive to barbel. Size 10 or 12 hooks, usually the excellent little Drennan Super Specialist are perfect for caster fishing, although they need regular inspection, as

*Peter with an 11lb
15oz barbel he
caught on the
Hampshire Avon
using sweetcorn.*

hookpoints are easily bent over on hard gravel, or just from hooking fish.

DAYS WITH SWEETCORN

It is not fashionable these days to fish with sweetcorn for barbel, but the bait must surely be due for something of a renaissance. I have used it as a summer bait for many years, and some of the biggest fish I have taken from the Avon and Stour have fallen to this bait. It is cheap, easy to use and absolutely deadly for barbel in the right circumstances.

The secret of corn fishing is to be the first to use it on a stretch, and also to realize when the fish have had enough of it, which does not take too long. By then, you should have caught your fish anyway! Although barbel will switch on to corn very quickly, it has a short useful life on a fishery. The fish soon learn to recognize it as a source of danger, and eventually will become terrified of even a few grains. It is actually quite a good barbel scarer to use if you want to keep them out of an area like a fallen tree or other snag they may be hiding in, as we discovered when first we began to fish the Ouse.

Four cans of corn and a similar amount of hemp or pellet is enough for a day, and it is always a good idea to bait a few swims in advance if you are concentrating on the stretch for a while. Another common mistake with corn is to overbait with it while fishing, because once fish are on to the bait they will be perfectly capable of seeking out and finding a single grain, even in coloured water or in low-light conditions. The corn they ate a few days or hours previously is very often the corn that has done the spadework for you. A bright yellow patch on the river-bed can cause alarm to even the hungriest barbel, and the trick is to give them enough to get them actively searching for the next crunchy morsel, but not so much as to make it a spoilt-for-choice situation! Fishing with corn enables a fairly mobile approach if need be, and with fish that are just getting used to it the response from them can be immediate.

I well remember one hot August fishing an Avon sidestream that was reputed to hold a few doubles. In sidestreams or small rivers that are heavily fished, the barbel soon become very private, and spend much of their time hiding in weed, under the bank or under trees.

The pressure of angling changes their behaviour significantly, and is one reason why I am in favour of disallowing night fishing on such small waters, as well as giving the fish an annual respite from our attentions in the form of the Close Season. These fish knew when they were being fished for, and responded by going into the weed and staying there for long periods, only emerging a few times a day to peck nervously at the little patch of hemp and red corn I had laid out for them. The dace and small chub that had no fear of me were still keen to eat anything I provided, however, and another advantage of corn now came into play. It is quite resistant to the attentions of small fish, and even a single grain, admittedly of the largest variety, can be fished for a long time without being whittled away by them. Caster and maggot is brilliant for working fish up into a feeding frenzy, and works well when you are fishing for numbers of active barbel and only a few nuisance fish.

When you are trying to tempt one or two barbel from a swim full of hungry tiddlers, it is often necessary to stick a bait on the bottom for some time and leave it there until the barbel decides to find the time to pay a visit. Such was the case with these sidestream barbel. Only occasionally would they reverse from the weed, have a bit of a munch, then go back to their sanctuary. A single grain of red corn, hair-rigged on a

twelve, was needed to fool them, and I had to plop a big bomb with a really short hook length right up into the tail of the weed, and wait for hours between fish. Hard work, but worth it. The fish would hook themselves and shoot upstream into the weed, then would reluctantly emerge, still kicking and fighting after a few minutes' pumping, in a cloud of silt and ripped-up weed. You never knew how big they were until the last seconds of the fight, and sometimes a solid, determined 7-pounder you were certain was a double would take you by surprise, and the bigger fish were actually easier to extract.

They say that the only place where success comes before work is in the dictionary, but there are occasions when a bit of luck can be yours, and the instant attraction of corn can result in a big fish coming your way, perhaps undeservedly, on the first cast. I had known about some big fish on a popular stretch of the Avon for a couple of years, but had been reluctant to have a go for them for a variety of reasons, not least because the swims were near to a holiday camp and often frequented by walkers, swimmers, dogs, boats and canoes.

I chose a dull, wet, drizzly day for my first visit, in the hope that some peaceful fishing was likely. A main attraction of the Avon is that there are long stretches of private estate water where even other anglers are rare, for fishing amongst noisy holiday-makers is not what I welcome.

The river here was uncharacteristically deep and slow, and with the low light levels spotting any fish seemed very unlikely. I walked the stretch from top to bottom, and was less than impressed. It was either too deep to see in or very shallow and weedy. There was one swim that seemed reasonable though, where the weedy water deepened off and there was a fairly fast, deep, clear run under the bank. A most convenient holly tree with one good stout branch

A beautiful 12lb 10oz barbel taken on sweetcorn, from the Hampshire Avon.

leaned out over the water, and there was even a place to fish from just off the foot-path where I was not going to get pestered or run over by a mountain bike.

I was still not keen. I had been mugged of some hooks by several surly youngsters on holiday from Rotherham, an elderly couple out walking had collared me and told me their life story in a very slow and tedious manner, and a pack of Labradors were trying to eat my rucksack. I half-heartedly threw a tin of corn and a few handfuls of hemp by hand into the weed above the drop off, and climbed the tree to escape my tormentors.

My mind began to clear, and so did the river. Weedcutting upstream had been sending down clouds of silt and rafts of cut weed, another reason for my lack of confidence or enthusiasm to fish this accursed bit of river. The holidaymakers were off for tea, and the swim below started to look more appealing as the clarity improved and I could make out a few features on the bottom. I could see where my corn and hemp had collected, as a few very large roach were drifting about and upending gently to savour the odd grain. Two of the fish were enormous, probably around 3lb in weight. I made a promise to myself to come back in the winter and try for them.

I stretched out full length on the branch, and strained my eyes to see across the river, looking for any sign of a barbel. I saw none – not even a chub, which was no problem, because chub are the real curse of the Avon corn fisher. They love corn and will eat it until they are literally sick, they will not even be put off it by being caught either, and come back time and time again to eat the corn designed to attract and feed barbel.

I took off my sunglasses, wiped them clean, and my polarized gaze returned to the baited patch beneath the branch. A huge barbel was sending up clouds of silt as it rooted around, gobbling up the corn and hemp that I had so carelessly tossed in a few minutes earlier. I actually watched him spot a little collection of corn grains, swim over and suck them in, then saw his gills working eagerly as he crunched them up in his throat teeth. He spat out a few bits of gravel, then drifted idly backward downstream beneath me, and melted into the shadowy deeps. I was down the tree in an instant, hastily set up a rod, and after a quick check to see that the barbel had not yet returned, I clumsily and hurriedly bait-dropped some more corn and hemp onto the edge of the drop off.

A simple running ledger, 2oz bomb, and a nice, long tail to a size 6, and three big fat grains of corn were soon cautiously lowered into position, and the rod top buried under the water, just about touching the bottom. The drifting weed was a constant nightmare.

This barbel was switched on to corn, his eyes were corn-yellow; he thought it was his birthday. Barely had five minutes passed before the rod walloped round and I was attached to a big barbel, the first cast on a new fishery. I got my feet wet as I stood out in the shallow water trying to keep this fish away from the near bank that was festooned with tree roots and what looked like old wooden fence posts or pilings. It just swam off downstream and simply would not stop; and there was no way I could follow, as the bank downstream was heavily wooded. Finally it stopped and sat, almost unmoving in the deep and not so slow water twenty yards below me.

Persuading a big, heavy barbel directly back upstream was not going to be easy. I was already standing, unsteadily on loose gravel, up to my knees in the river, holding the rod at arm's length and desperate that the fish did not snag me under that near bank woodwork. I tried to prepare myself mentally for the loss of this fish as things did not seem favourable. I put the rod under the water, and just maintained firm pressure, in the way that I was used to bringing grayling back upstream against a heavy flow. Raising the rod is futile in such circumstances, and the same with barbel. You have to keep the rod as low as possible, or they just keep swimming down with the current further away from you.

I scraped the bottom a few times with the rod tip, but after firm, constant pressure had been kept on the fish, it swam slowly and ever so grudgingly back up into the swim. It looked enormous, with a big bold head and thick shoulders combined with a length that told me it had to be a 14-pounder. A couple of times it just turned its flank to me, hung in the current and swam irresistibly across the river and under the weed, with the almost leisurely strokes of its great paddle of a tail.

Even at 13lb 10oz, it was a monster of a fish, and one of my favourite barbel of all time, despite being a bit of a sucker for corn that day. It was a recognizable fish, with a badly marked flank, and was taken at 14lb 11oz later on that season. We all deserve a jammy capture every now and then, and there is no point in pretending that all our fish are extracted by pure unadulterated skill and design. Sometimes a big fish helps us out, and just jumps on the end, so why not admit it!

That capture was getting on for twelve years ago, when I used corn in various forms and with a range of presentations for a good deal of my summer fishing, and when I think back it was a pretty productive bait not only for barbel, but for chub and roach. Only last year, I decided to try it again in one of my old haunts above Ibsley, and after coming across a nice-looking fish in a deep run right under my feet, I droppered in two tins' worth, with a generous helping of hemp and koi pellet for good measure. I had spent much of the day wandering about, baiting likely looking areas on a virtually unfished length of bank, and discovered a small group of fish sitting just under the surface on top of a bed of cabbages, underwater lily leaves. The only fishable spot was a tiny patch of sand just upstream of them and under the bank in about six feet of water. This was where I would see if I could reinvent corn fishing, and to where my bed of bait would hopefully end up attracting those wild-looking barbel, one of which looked a good double.

The next morning I was straining my eyes, standing on tiptoe, to see if the yellow blobs of sprinkled corn were doing their job. I had sprinkled in a few grains by hand a little upstream, not wishing to baitdrop onto the heads of any fish that might be in the swim. The corn drifted exactly into place in a most satisfying manner; I had forgotten how easy it was to loose-feed the stuff by hand once you have the measure of the flow and depth.

From directly above, the fish that I saw move into the swim looked massive, with a wide piggy head and broad shoulders, and one by one it hoovered up the corn grains until the one with a hook in took it by surprise, and the centrepin screamed as the biggest barbel of the group buried itself in the cabbage patch. It turned out to be a 9-pounder with a big head and a slender body, at least 12in long, but it reminded me that the old yellow peril still has some uses in modern barbel fishing. Two other fish were to fall for the corn that day, fat little 7-pounders that had not been caught before.

If nothing else, corn is a cheap way of feeding up or finding barbel that are perhaps unused to it or have forgotten about it, and it remains a nice medium-sized durable hook-bait that can still be fished on top of other particles as a change bait. Corn can be fished as a big bright hook-bait of four, five, six or more grains glued together, or as a single tiny speck, hair-rigged or sidehooked, popped up with foam or the excellent artificials, coloured and flavoured, fed in by the bucket load or flicked in surreptitiously, little and often. A truly versatile bait. You can always eat it when you are peckish, too. There are always a few tins of supermarket corn in the car, along with some of the flavoured and dyed stuff.

AUGUST ON THE OUSE

When first I fished the Ouse above Bedford I was struck by how similar it was in nature to the Stour, especially the stretches below Newport Pagnell. The river is like a little Stour, with a nice flow and some clarity, and good thick beds of bulrush and streamer weed, also being quite gravelly in places. I first fished it at Turvey, in the company of Stef Horak, whom I had taught to barbel fish some years earlier, and was fortunate enough to catch an 11-pounder on that first visit.

A local angler seemed astounded that the fish had been caught in daylight, so used was he to night fishing the stretch. If there is any species of coarse fish that does not need fishing for at night, then it is the barbel, and Ouse barbel are no different from barbel elsewhere. Some people may choose or prefer to catch them in the dark, but they do not really need to.

The Weir Swim at Adams Mill. There are five doubles unseen below the surface, including a 15lb 12oz fish that was caught on the day that this photograph was taken.

This first Ouse barbel took a tiny bit of Pepperami fished over a light sprinkling of trout pellet and hemp, in a narrow channel alongside one of those nice big beds of bulrush. That fish not only sparked off a real interest in Ouse barbel, it was while I was fishing that stretch that another local angler came down the bank and complained how he had struggled to catch barbel from a whole shoal of doubles at somewhere called Adams Mill.

The next day we were walking the bank at Adams, and close inspection from both banks, in bright sunlight was not very revealing. We did not see a single barbel, and although not many anglers were present, those that there were had little to report. I was astounded at how tiny the

river was, and it took some believing that a 14-pounder and a few 13-pounders had already been out that season.

The next day we returned, determined to find those barbel for ourselves. A few fish were spotted, some in a depression upstream of the bridge, and a few small fish under a bush on the far bank. They were quite shy of corn and hemp, the only bait we had brought with us, and it was clear that the fish had seen corn, meat and pellet before, and the low, warm conditions of a typical August were not ideal in any event. I think Stef had lost a fish that day, and I blanked, but we were learning about the swims and realizing that these fish were fairly pressured and expert at hiding themselves away.

It had rained hard the previous evening and that afternoon had been wet and stormy, but the forecast was for an improvement, and on the third day I returned with a gallon of maggots and the hope that the extra water would freshen things up a bit. The river had indeed risen a few inches, yet retained its clarity. As I peered into the swim I had fished so fruitlessly the day before I was amazed to see a shoal of double-figure barbel, probably six or seven big fish swimming in mid-water in the flow of cool, oxygenated water that was now coursing through a previously limpid pool. Stef and I always called it the Corner Pool, and it no doubt has a proper name, but that pool will always hold fond memories for me.

These Ouse barbel had not really had the maggot treatment, and in those days they were not that tackle shy. The pool was not easy to fish by any means, with no obvious killing zone, so I carefully bait-dropped a couple of pints at the head of the swim, just behind some clay boulders, added a bit of hemp, and watched their response. There were soon four doubles standing on their heads, digging around for the maggots, almost fighting for position.

They settled into a routine of swimming round the pool in rotation, but as I kept up a regular feeding pattern of four droppers every half hour and no casting in, they became more and more confident, filtering in from the left, often head to tail as they started to queue up for the bait. Maggots are unbeatable at times for barbel, and it seems to be becoming a bit of a lost art, as they can seem expensive and inconvenient at times. Knowing when not to use them is the key. It is entirely possible to waste a gallon or more of maggots just feeding small fish, or barbel that are not there, but when they are used on the right day in the right way you can empty a swim, and the big fish will fall for them too.

These fish had been stimulated by the fresh water, and they were also not used to heavy feeding with maggots and soon got switched on in no uncertain manner. It was possible to bait up almost directly under the rod top if I stretched out, and consequently a hook-bait of hair-rigged maggots could be lowered into exactly the right spot each time.

I had four doubles in that session, including my first really big fish from the Ouse. It seemed to appear from nowhere, a shape more substantial even than the big brown shapes that were ghosting about in the deep, and now slightly coloured water, under my feet. More nervous and cautious than the rest, it took until late afternoon before it made a mistake, and the rod hooped round once more to result in an unusually slow, unyielding force. This was a fish in a different league from the rest and I was soon witness to a great bronze flank showing itself off to me, as the biggest barbel I had seen in some time just turned gently in the current and ponderously swam across the little pool.

At 14lb 3oz that fish is not my biggest, but remains my favourite Ouse barbel. It was a young, short, fat solid fish, with a small head and a bulldog build that surely meant that further growth was possible. It did come out later that year to Adrian Busby, at 15lb 10oz, but died the following June.

I now have a cast of that fish on the wall in the lounge, and every time I look at it I am reminded of those great days at Adams Mill before it was lost by the local club and became syndicated. Fishing like that could not be kept secret, and it was inevitable that it would receive an undue amount of attention. When people were forming queues at the gate as we were leaving in the evening it was time to try elsewhere.

We did get a couple of years of fairly quiet and productive fishing, however, and

Pete's favourite Ouse barbel, a magnificent 14lb 3oz specimen caught on maggots at the Corner Swim at Adams Mill.

it was maggot or caster fished craftily in the swims and conditions that suited them that did the damage.

One of the last times we fished it, I found a group of fish in the weir, where they were not often seen. Like the Corner Pool, there was no obvious place to fish, and the barbel were really edgy and prone to hiding under some duckweed on the inaccessible far bank for most of the time. If you could get them to swim out from cover and down to the tail of the pool, they were likely to get themselves downstream

of your feed and take an interest. Flicking a few grains of corn, which they hated the sight of, or the odd pebble, was enough to send them out for a swim round, and by the end of a long, hot day they were out and feeding for short spells on a patch of maggot and hemp I had been topping up virtually all day.

Even when particle fishing, on difficult waters like Adams it was required that you sometimes did not actually cast in and fish for several hours. The way to catch those fish was to continually feed them, cajole

47

them into a slowly but surely increasing sense of confidence, gradually luring them into your baited area until they lost their nervousness and made a mistake. The mistake that you can make, and I sometimes did, was to rush things and scare the fish off by fishing for them too quickly. A badly timed or splashy bit of baitdropping or miscast could send the fish off and out of the swim for the rest of the day. It means that you must spend a lot of time just watching the fish, judging their reactions, seeing if they are feeding in that persistent head down, tail up, manner and pounding their noses into the gravel, losing enough caution to make themselves catchable.

On this occasion, there were three big fish feeding for short periods of a couple of minutes but no longer, and not long enough for a bait to survive the attention of the hordes of silver fish that were in the weirpool, not to mention the chub. As the sun dropped behind the woods at my back, it was time for a last-ditch effort, that is, the introduction of the bulk of my remaining bait. This is a trick that can either pay off or backfire, and thankfully this time it paid off handsomely. In went four pints of maggots, and I watched in trepidation as the group of fish moved up on the bait for what was probably the last time that day. I had already plonked a big feeder full of maggots onto the killing zone.

I am sure that this one particular fish had not been in the swim before, or it just looked bigger than the rest in the half light, but I shall not forget the sight of that big, broad barbel bulldozing two mere 13-pounders out of the way as it suddenly developed maggot fever. It was hammering into the gravel, sucking up maggots, sifting the grubs and hemp from the silty bottom when its head jerked suddenly to one side as the sharp, little hook pricked those blubbery lips, and it shot off across the pool into the nasty rocky area on the far bank.

The fight was the slow and dogged, typical of the biggest barbel, when you constantly wonder where they get the strength from to make yet another powerful run under the weed or across the current. Those arm-aching, knee-trembling long, agonized fights are memorable, but at the time you just want it to be all over. The size of that fish was not truly apparent until I tried to lift it out of the water, and its bulk became obvious as it lay like a big common carp in the net. This was The Pope, and I had in fact caught it the previous year at 15lb 5oz. At 15lb 12oz it was a respectable summer weight, and still my biggest barbel. This fish went on to gain a few more pounds and I think is the current record. It was not an easy fish to forget.

Another swim that lent itself to the maggot, we named Two Trees, and here the barbel were holed up under a far bank raft when in residence, which really depended on water levels. They were at home the first and only time I fished it, and it was the close, intimate, really exciting sort of barbel fishing, that can make small river fishing enjoyable, yet sometimes questionable. It was clear from observation from the far bank that there were fish under the raft, and a constant trickle of maggots soon had them actively feeding, but not willing to move from cover. It was possible to bait drop feed right at the head of the raft, and as usual I fed them for a while to ensure they were in a state of near frenzy before I cast in.

With practice and care, it was possible to drop a big feeder of maggots so it literally bounced off the leading branch of the tree, hold it back ever so slightly, and allow a big bunch of maggots on a 2ft tail to drift under the raft. Holding the rod was not needed to detect the bites, but only to ensure that you were in instant contact with the fish as soon as they hooked themselves. They had nowhere to go other than

A 14lb 8oz barbel taken on maggots from under a bush at Adams Mill.

further under the bush, and the rod top was immediately lowered beneath the water to play the fish out under maximum pressure without snagging in the branches.

I only lost one, I think, that took me a bit by surprise, but I well remember watching a 14-pounder emerging from the gloom under that tree and on the end of my line that enraged a passing swan so much that the bird tried to attack the barbel. It reared up, hissing aggressively and flapping its wings, and was making lunges at the puzzled fish as I desperately tried to keep the line out of its way. Big fish look even bigger in a tiny stream such as the Ouse is at Adams, and the swan may have mistaken it for a pike, or simply just another animal; swans are pretty intolerant creatures. Luckily it lost interest when the barbel charged back under the bush, and I eventually landed it.

I do not mind fishing under trees and rafts, or in thick weed for barbel. These snags are rarely as bad as they look and you soon find out if fish are landable, or you should have the sense not to fish the obvious no-hopers in the first place. The next time I went to that swim, however, it had been fished by someone apparently incapable of casting in. The marginal reeds had been turned into a muddy quagmire as this person had clearly constantly waded in and out of the water to place his bait by pushing his rod under the bush, not being content to draw the fish out. I think that is going a bit far, and much prefer to fish from the bank, and I draw the line at shoving baits up under trees. You might as well put on a wetsuit and swim with the barbel, inserting your hook into their mouths when they open them! Wading into snags is a poor substitute for skill and patience, but difficult to regulate against. There is always someone more desperate than the rest, and these small river barbel are quite at risk from overfishing or exploitation as it is. They generally learn to avoid the desperadoes, and often just get fed up and swim off somewhere else if they can.

Summer fishing at Adams epitomized the combination of careful fish observation and patient, planned and well-timed

A 12-pounder with classic colouration taken on casters from Adams Mill.

baiting so necessary to fishing with maggots in the most effective way. It was likely that if you managed to get into a swim with some fish in residence, you could almost guarantee two or more fish in a day, and at Adams they could all be double-figure fish.

I reckon at that time there were twenty or more doubles in a few hundred yards of river, but they were pretty mobile and could be in the hole above the bridge one day, and fifty yards down in The Depression, or upstream in the weir the next. Once you had chosen your swim, it was a case of watch and wait and bait up, wait some more, or check out a Plan B swim just in case your Plan A failed, as it sometimes did.

As the fishery became more popular, the chances of moving swim were less and less likely, so swim selection at the start of the day was quite a nerve-racking affair. The wrong choice could spell disaster, condemning you to a frustrating, fishless day spent photographing other people's barbel.

Too much fishing under pressure like that is no good for you in the long term, so we only ever made occasional visits there in any event. The last time we drove past, there were five white vans waiting in the entrance half an hour before opening time. It was time to move on.

DAYS ON THE KENNET

The first time I fished the Kennet was in the company of Ian Welch, who owed me a favour, as I had just recently guided him to his best ever fish from the Avon. He was rightly delighted with a 12-pounder from the swim I had put him in, but I insisted that I would simply be satisfied with a barbel of any size from his home river. Ian took me on a tour of a stretch he knew well, showed me the best swim, and even gave me a little bag of the bait that he had been using to good effect that season. I was very taken with this bit of river. It was full of features, with a good range of depths and lots of overhanging trees. Ian advised me that the fish were in the process of working their way downstream from the weir at the top of the fishery, and were now well distributed. They did favour any swims with cover, which is to be expected. The swim he put me in was well known, a fair way upstream of a big snag in the form of a submerged tree, and needed a long cast downstream and to the far bank.

I thought I knew better, and decided to try and draw the fish up to a patch of hemp and caster under the far bank. I tried a cast down to Ian's hotspot while he was there, paying lip service to his advice, and trying to cast a heavy backlead as well as a 3oz in line lead twenty yards downstream with an underarm swing. The leads crashed into the water in a total mess and in quite the wrong place. Ian looked at me with that polite, blank smile that people use when they think you are doing something stupid but are too polite to say so. As he walked off back upstream to his swim, I sat and pondered, remaining determined to catch using the particle method rather than employing the established method of roving with the big lumps of paste, boilie or pellet that I was advised was only worth doing in the evenings in any case.

Ian had taken two 11-pounders before I had even settled in to my fishing, and I eventually followed his advice and was rewarded with a sprightly 7-pounder within minutes of casting his recommended bait to his recommended spot. I failed miserably to draw any fish up to my baited particle patch, and was frustrated by the huge numbers of dace, roach and small chub that were having a fine time gobbling up my rapidly decreasing bait reserves. In the end I had a couple of fish on my first visit,

and was intrigued and interested in the river, eager to return and learn some more. It can be foolish to ignore local knowledge as a matter of principle, and although my plan to take that place apart with particles failed at the first attempt, I knew that if I could get those barbel introduced to caster or maggot they would be like lambs to the slaughter.

The real problem with that bit of Kennet was that although it was a small, shallow river the pale grey discolouration that was always present meant that you could not see the fish, and fishing blind with particles is trickier than feeding up and being able to watch how the fish respond. The lack of clarity is apparently due to a combination of increased boat traffic on the canalized sections that interrupt the proper river, and the inevitable algal blooms from our warmer, more nitrified groundwater. Combine low summer flows and hotter than average summer weather and this turbidity is now a permanent feature of much of the Kennet. Whatever the cause, it makes it hard to see what the barbel are doing, or even if there are any fish in your swim at all.

The next time I fished the swim a little differently, baiting up heavily with maggot in the middle of the river, out in open water but much closer to the snag that the fish were gathered under. Much heavier baiting was needed, and six or seven droppers every half an hour was the minimum needed to both draw out the barbel and feed off the small fish. The maggots were presented on a short length of braid weighted down with a bigger than average swivel, to bomb the hook-bait down through the silver fish and nail it hard to the bottom.

Two of the hook-bait maggots were artificials, a soft version imported from the USA by Berkeley, I think. This ensured that when the barbel moved up there was still a takeable bait around! Artificials do have their place in such circumstances, and are handy when nuisance fish are merely an occasional pest. An unrelenting presence of small fish and crushed baits every single cast are invariably an indication that the barbel are not going to ever arrive! It is a hard call deciding on whether to stick it out and try to feed them off, or give up and try elsewhere. This day I knew the barbel were not far away, and tolerated small fish activity until that moment came when the rod top signalled some slow, lurching spring-back line bites, and hook-baits were reeled in, firm and wriggly and untouched. This was a sure sign that the barbel were moving in, and it was not too long before the rod would slam round and the pin protest loudly as a surprised barbel headed home to the snag.

That first summer we usually ended up bagging six or seven fish throughout the day, getting the best from the swim and were off home before the mosquitoes that plagued the place got too active.

Caster and hemp/pellet mix became more standard than maggot the following year, and I had some of my best sport in recent years on that bit of river. One of the most daunting looking swims on that stretch was under a tree that had fallen right across the river, soon to be removed by the EA as a flood defence measure, I was told. There were certainly a whole bunch of barbel underneath it, and my good friend Dave Charles generously alerted me to the swim, having taken good bags of up to nine fish in an evening. I only fished it three times, but had over thirty barbel out of it, including a brace of 13-pounders in one day.

At short range you can bait up with deadly accuracy, and by maintaining continual baiting in the same spot the barbel under that tree were subjected to the irresistible pulling power of particles. They needed time to build up confidence, however, and it would sometimes be half an hour before the first bite. It could be that they were dotted about further downstream than we imagined, and gained in confidence as they increased in numbers.

It was possible to dispense with a feeder, and I soon became adept at dropping an in-line lead and a very short tail, with a backlead to pin down the line onto the

A Kennet 13-pounder. The swim in which this fish was caught also produced three different thirteens and a 12lb 14oz for Pete in three visits.

bottom in what I thought was a pretty small area.

I had noticed that liners were enough to scare the fish off for a while, and a half ounce bullet three feet from the lead was enough to prevent any further line bites and subsequent nervousness.

The use of a centrepin is perfect for these close-range tactics, especially when you cannot afford to give an inch more line than you have to. With a pin you can not only give line a quarter of an inch at a time, with ultimate control, you can retrieve it with unrelenting power and efficiency. There is no need to pump, as with a fixed spool, you can actually winch a fish toward you, winding in line with total authority.

There is an almost inexplicable pleasure in playing fish on the pin, and I use one whenever I can nowadays. Those jazzy reels with all the handles do look nice, but I am unashamedly old-fashioned, I suppose, and a Mitchell 300, perhaps more aged than I am, will provide for me all that I need from a reel when I am not using a centrepin. The battles with those Kennet barbel under that tree were pretty one-sided nevertheless, and I only lost one, which took me by surprise and got a bit too far into the woodwork. I was impressed by the strength, fitness and condition of the Kennet barbel, but the fact that they were living in semi-darkness in a grey-coloured river meant that their colouration was rather dull. They had a ghostly grey-white

A 12lb 15oz from the Kennet that was taken on maggots.

sheen, a sort of metallic lustre that I was not used to. When the bigger ones hove into view, as the inexorable pinpower brought them to the surface, they seemed like great ghost barbel, reluctant to be disturbed from their quiet life in the gloomy depths. Avon and Stour barbel are much nicer to look at, but then they live in brighter surroundings most of the time, I suppose.

The tree has gone now, and no doubt the barbel have scattered, which is just as well. I may well go back next year and try to find them, but there are other stretches of the Kennet I need to explore. It is a lovely river in the more natural reaches, I am told, and where weed is more widespread and the water clarity is better I can see some barbel; it is much better than fishing blind. So many rivers, so little time!

AUTUMNAL THOUGHTS

Those first hints of coolness, the mist-veiled threats of frost in the mornings, and loss of colour and vigour in the water weed is a sign that the barbel are either going to have a good feed up or switch off, depending on rainfall. The Stour can suffer badly from low water levels in the early autumn months, and without a good flood the river can be clear, cold and sad-looking, with the weed turning brown and soft and starting to break down and rot. The fishing is hard, as the oxygen levels probably drop and the fish become a bit listless and lacklustre. Their metabolism seems to slow down, they appear to just lie up and wait for rain, sensing the oncoming winter, but not yet stimulated to feed.

I had spent all morning watching a big fish drift aimlessly up and down one of the few patches of gravel not smothered in the grey-green silkweed that had built up in the summer months, and had not been

flushed away by rain or the actions of feeding fish. This was a great, lazy fish, a tiny bit interested in the specks of crumbled boilie I had so cautiously droppered into a narrow channel at the head of the swim. It would swim so slowly, creepily, up along the bottom to the baited area, show vague interest for a moment or two, then allow the now feeble current to carry it across and downstream again to the sanctuary of the bulrush roots on the opposite bank. I had been told by an earnest young converted carp angler I had met on the bank that day that barbel allow themselves to drift across swims in this fashion so as to detect any line in the swim, before they start to feed. Well, it is nice to credit them with such intelligence and intent, but I do not think that this is so. It is just the way they get around when they are feeling lazy, they just let the current do the work.

Sometimes they reverse grandly over weedbeds, making a big show of themselves before they effortlessly disappear from view, as if to say 'Look at me, you can't catch me and I want you to know it!' This barbel was doing this to me, showing off, almost pretending to be interested in feeding and trying to wind me up, swimming round and round and begging me to make a mistake.

The mistake would have been to put in more bait, to try and provoke a response. Maggots might have done the trick, but the disturbance on a single fish that seemed half-asleep already would probably have sent it packing. Some days you have to grit your teeth and rely on an accurately cast static bait that a half-interested fish should eventually pick up.

I guessed that if I kept my nerve and waited it out, this fish would be unable to resist the hair-rigged half boilie that was sitting so temptingly in the patch of crumbled bits of boilie and paste I had so cunningly prepared. The swarms of minnow would also have made short work of less robust particles. I reckon that the Stour minnows have some piranha genes in their ancestry. In the heat of the summer I had foolishly cooled my bare feet in a swim on the same stretch by walking in the shallows, and was astounded at how hard minnows can bite; they attacked my toes so ferociously I thought that crayfish were responsible to begin with, until I was able to peer in and see a shoal of these aggressive little fish trying to eat my feet. No wonder the boilies so often come back picked clean of the paste that I usually wrap around them.

Sitting and waiting with a hard but attractively flavoured good-quality bait had to pay off, but I was beginning to think that the big old barbel had won this little war of attrition when he suddenly woke up, made one last visit to the baited patch, finally sucked in that hook-bait, and dragged the rod round in a slow, powerful bite that meant he intended to keep on swimming.

As with some really big fish, the fight can be a short and disappointing affair, and this fish seemed a bit tired and disinterested in trying very hard. It was a most welcome monster nonetheless, and was the first of four 14-pounders I took from the stretch that autumn and winter. The others were to take a liking to Mr Baker's paste in more usual late-season conditions, when the river was pushing through at two or three feet above normal level, and a flush of warm water really gets the fish going.

Fishing a nice, big, smelly bait that the fish have got used to eating is the way to maximize catches, and with these baits I have found that results can be almost immediate. I usually fish four of five swims in a day if possible, expecting a response of some sort on the first or second cast. There is an eager expectation every time you up sticks and settle down in a new swim, and although I am not a fan of the constantly

roving approach for its own sake, I can see the attraction.

There are times when do you need to stay put, and you will catch more by being flexible in your approaches. It can take time for even a prebaited and prepared barbel to make up its mind, and I remember catching a big, solid hump-backed 14-pounder by staying in a swim for five hours, because for some reason I felt it was right. Perhaps the old sixth sense came into play, perhaps I was really feeling comfortable, but I would certainly not have caught it if I had moved after the usual hour or so.

These high-water conditions can be unbearable at times because of the constant stream of weed, sticks, logs and other debris that typify floodwater on the Stour and Avon. This is when the backlead comes into its own, and sometimes a 2oz flying lead as well as an extra ounce of lead slid down the line after casting is needed to keep the line on the bottom and away from that drifting weed that would otherwise make fishing impossible.

A knowledge of your stretch gained from summer observations is important here, and you must be sure that you are not casting into an old weedbed or worse. There are some old stumps, rocks and farm gates that it is as well to know about before you start casting in on this bit of the Stour, and the farm gate lost me a good fish on one occasion when I forgot about it.

There is no doubt that the current in the highest flood does not bother barbel; they do not generally move into slacks so as to avoid the extra flow in my experience, in fact they seem to relish it. Fishing through a slack into fast water is a sensible idea though, and helps to avoid the interminable drifting weed.

These late-season floods are becoming more prevalent, it seems, and there is no doubt that they enable barbel to move quite long distances. Some very identifiable fish on the Stour appeared to move several miles last season, and the many weirs on the river were no obstacle to them. Barbel appear to be as powerful in terms of musculature as salmon, and could probably traverse any weir on the river in normal conditions if the fancy took them. When the entire river takes on the appearance of a lake, and the weirs are invisible to us they are likely to be inconsequential to the barbel. Perhaps this explains why some fish can seem to disappear from a stretch, only to pop up again a few years later.

WINTRY RAMBLINGS

True winter fishing is not as predictable as those first autumnal flushes, and only a few die-hards will fish for barbel in any conditions throughout the colder months. Most winter fish come out when there has been a sustained rise in temperature and accompanying warm rain, and the boilie and paste technique really comes into its own here. Some people will remain devoted to the reliable old luncheon meat in its various forms, and it must be said that barbel have been eating it for years and will no doubt continue to do so.

I still think the well-designed pastes and some more highly flavoured boilies should have an edge over meat from the tin, and by the time you have dyed and fried and smothered your meat in flavours it is no longer meat. It is easily possible to obtain bait with a better texture, content and considered flavour and taste. However, if you persist in using what you have confidence in, and feed and present it correctly, you will continue to catch on whatever bait you choose. Barbel do not read the books or articles, and I have long maintained that they will eat anything if you throw enough in. The best baits will simply need less thrown in to begin with!

Rising coloured water is not a favourite situation for me, but those times when the rod has been wrenched round by an unseen but well imagined fat winter barbel can be really exciting. Catching them in those nice warm spells when persistent, long-awaited south-westerly rain has flushed through for a few days and woken up the otherwise torpid fish is what brings a host of barbellers out on to the bank, and the rivers are sometimes busier than during the summer. Sorting out where the fish are likely to be when you have difficulty getting to the bank yourself is a problem with winter fishing, but the joy of that feeling of surprise and elation when a greedy barbel ends up being where you hoped it would be is worth the effort. It must be admitted that the fish are likely to be at their heaviest after Christmas but I do not understand, or envy, those who only ever fish for barbel when they are at their prize-winning biggest. They are missing out on a lot of good fishing, and the things they learn in the summer when fishing for lesser fish, will stand them in good stead when the floodwater arrives in February and they are working out where to go

On the Avon in particular, the summery swims can become unfishable and unapproachable when there is extra water on the river, and I well remember standing and looking at one of my favourite summer haunts in January, when the normally placid flow had been replaced by a boiling, swirling torrent full of a messy mixture of dead leaves, sticks and drifting weed that would have needed a pound of lead to hold bottom for any length of time. It would have meant wading out and sitting in water to fish as well. Barbel do not mind fast currents, but the ferocious boiling maelstrom my swim had turned into could not possibly hold any fish in those conditions. Where were they?

A big-finned, old 11-pounder caught on the Avon.

Fifty yards upstream, was a normally shallow, clear, gravelly area that was sometimes used by that barbel shoal for spawning, but was not much of a swim in times of normal flow. I waded up to it, where the bank was higher and fishing could be quite comfortable.

The water was now 18in deeper, still very fast, but the surface was urgently smooth, and there was also a little lay-by slack where the rod tip could be buried out from the incessant hurtling swirl of drifting debris. Had the barbel moved up here, or had one of the bigger than average fish that I knew were in this area taken up

residence? I bunged in perhaps thirty or forty boilies, no more than one good handful, and resolved to return the next weekend if the weather held.

It remained warm and wet, and the next week I was there with some boilies and fresh paste, full of excited anticipation. Nobody fished here much in the summer, let alone the winter, so the worry of getting the swim was not detracting from my feeling of confident wellbeing. The water was even higher, and had a brownish tinge that is quite rare on the Avon, as it never really gets very coloured, or stays coloured for very long.

A 4oz lead with a double backlead was needed to combat the current and drifting weed, but the barbel were there, and a big 12-pounder and some lesser doubles were the reward for braving the conditions and risking it in a new swim. How they fought too, more dogged and determined than in the summer, holding station in the raging current, and at times swimming upstream against all odds. Battles like that can warm you up nicely on those cold, wet and windy days when the slow, sultry relaxing days of summer seem a world away.

There is always the next barbel season to look forward to!

CONCLUSION

There is no right or wrong way to catch barbel, no best or worst method, or most questionable technique. There is only the way that you most enjoy catching them, and as long as there is no harm to the fish, or genuine upset to your fellow anglers, no lack of proper respect for fish or fisherman, then we should all fish as we like, when and where we like best, and treasure the thrills and joy that barbel fishing can bring.

Barbel are now distributed so widely that most anglers no longer need to make pilgrimages to the old Meccas of the southern rivers, the old spiritual homes of barbel fishing. The greatest and the smallest of our rivers are now home to increasingly large barbel populations as well as to some huge fish. Despite this wealth of fishing, we all run the risk of getting too set in our ways, of sticking to our favourite, tried and tested methods, perhaps to the detriment of our fishing. Making that mistake is probably an inevitability at one time or another, and we have almost all certainly been guilty of it.

The secret of sustained enthusiasm and success must surely be in being prepared to recognize your mistakes, change your ingrained attitudes and simply aim to keep on learning and, of course, catching more barbel. Keeping one or two steps ahead of the fish and indeed other barbel fishermen is challenging, and the failures are as valuable as the successes. You can learn an awful lot by catching nothing but next time you are out on the bank, the thought and perhaps humble consideration that you put into explaining your lack of fish, could well result in the change of tactics that results in an exceptional, dreamed-of catch.

I shall certainly keep fishing with as much of an open mind as I can manage, and try to maintain that eagerness to catch new barbel in new ways, for when I stop learning I know that the enjoyment will stop too.

Respect the barbel, respect each other and enjoy!

OPPOSITE: Pete returns an 11lb 15oz fish that was recaptured two years later at 14lb 11oz.

Guy Robb

Guy Robb was born in 1960 and has been fishing since he was ten years of age. The first barbel he caught weighed 9lb and was from the Royalty on the Hampshire Avon. Guy has also caught barbel in Spain and France and has been fishing for mahseer in India. His favourite rivers are the Thames and the Cauvery in Southern India.

Guy, is a specialist in clear-water fishing, held the British Barbel record with a 17lb 6¾oz fish caught on the Great Ouse in March 2000. He also held the British record for the biggest brace of barbel (15lb 4oz and 15lb, 13 March 1999). Moreoever, in one week he caught barbel from the Great Ouse weighing 18lb 10oz, 17lb 14oz, 16lb 8oz and 15lb 4oz. In addition, he caught two 14-pounders and two 13-pounders in a single afternoon. He has caught dozens of barbel over 14lb and has caught 13lb fish from the Bristol Avon and the River Colne together with many double-figure fish from the Ouse, Kennet, Dorset Stour, Hampshire Avon, the Thames, Lee, Severn and Teme. His personal best barbel is 18lb 10oz from the Great Ouse.

Guy starred in the best-selling barbel video entitled Barbel Up Close and Personal. He is a fishing rod designer, has contributed to fishing magazines and newspapers, and is a campaigner to keep the close season on rivers.

Guy with The Pope, the then (March 2000) Great Ouse river record barbel.

3 Large Recaptured Barbel

by Guy Robb

INTRODUCTION

In this part of the book I will cover how I fish for some of the biggest and most pursued barbel in the country and I will try to describe how I think that they have adapted their behaviour to avoid constant recapture. In order to do this I will look at clear-water fishing because it enables me to observe the barbel's reaction to both my tackle and baits. Over the years I have learnt to adapt my tackle and baits to be more effective at attracting and catching these highly prized fish and I will share this information with you later on. Also I have included fish observation and swim location, as they are fundamental to my angling success.

Barbel fishing has been my passion for nearly thirty years and I actively seek out information that may help me in my quest to know more about the species. In my search for knowledge, I have read many books about barbel fishing and other types of angling, to see how different methods and rigs could be used to improve my catch rate. Also, friends and acquaintances whom I have met on the riverbank have greatly influenced the way I fish today, with their freely given advice, enthusiasm and good humour.

People go barbel fishing for many different reasons. A growing number of anglers, myself included, spend a great deal of time tracking down the bigger fish while others are more than content to catch barbel of any size. Before we look at some of the fishing techniques that I use, I think it would be helpful to explain my theory on why I believe some of our very big barbel are changing their feeding patterns and behaviour in order to evade recapture.

Barbel fishing has changed beyond recognition over the last few years. When I first started out, multiple catches of barbel were the norm from venues like the Kennet, the Hampshire Avon and the Stour. The barbel shoals were vast and could be caught on simple baits using crude and basic tacts; such was the competition for food. The situation on many of our rivers today could not be more different. In the last ten years, there has been an apparent downturn in the barbel population. While the numbers of fish have fallen, their average size has grown. This has attracted more specialist anglers, particularly from the carp world, bringing with them improvements in tackle and bait, that, in turn has played a significant part in the rise of recaptures.

On our noted big fish waters, the recapture rate is so high that I suspect all the resident barbel, view their every meal as another photo opportunity. The more identifiable fish have even been given pet names – not really a good thing, but a fact none the less. It is hard to understand that in the face of such recapture, the fish have become wary of certain baits, tatics and presentation. Make any mistakes in your fishing approach and you may not catch at all – you almost need a science degree to get a bite. Some anglers are in denial that we are all fishing for barbel that may have been caught dozens of times before. Only those that are prepared to accept this as reality will make the necessary changes in their fishing approach, to stay one step ahead of those wary, big fish.

In my opinion, some of the main reasons for this drop in barbel population are water abstraction, over-zealous flood-relief programmes and a lack of seasonal rainfall. When the rain does arrive, it all comes at once during the winter, causing widespread flooding. Our once fast-flowing rivers now resemble drainage ditches due to a lack of flow during spring and summer. This reduction in water flow has caused barbel-spawning grounds to silt up, having a negative effect on barbel reproduction. On southern rivers, the population has dwindled so much that they have to be artificially stocked with barbel. The Environment Agency has even stocked the Hampshire Avon with fingerlings from their fish farms. Things must be bad if you need to stock the Avon.

Less numbers of barbel in the rivers means more food for the remaining fish. The remaining fish have grown to weights once thought impossible, with the largest fish approaching 20lb. Double-figure barbel are increasingly common. On some rivers in the south, they are now considered as average-sized fish. This may be great news for specimen hunters, but a worry for the future of barbel fishing. Another reason for the fishes' weight gain is the increased use of high nutritional value baits like boilies, pastes and pellets. These baits are highly calorific and contain high protein levels, vitamins and minerals that the barbel find irresistible.

OBSERVATION AND LOCATION

My fishing has mainly revolved around finding and catching big barbel in areas of rivers, often ignored by other anglers. Looking for big barbel requires a lot of time and effort, especially if the river contains a low head of fish. Many rivers run gin-clear during the summer and location can be quite easy. You will need polarizing sunglasses as these remove surface glare from the water, enabling you to see into the river. Some rivers have a slight tinge of colour that can make observation difficult but not impossible.

If you spend lots of time looking for barbel, your eyes become trained in spotting fish even if the water is not crystal-clear. In these conditions, observation is about looking for shapes and shadows in likely looking areas of the river. Never ignore a gut feeling; intuition and instinct play a huge part in my fishing. Snags, weedbeds, overhanging trees, rushes and deeper water are all potential fish-holding areas. However these areas will be heavily fished, as they are obvious to all barbel anglers, and therefore not the best places to find the biggest fish.

As I am looking for very big barbel, one of the first things that I do, is to select the right fishery. Selecting a fishery used to be qutie difficult, as local anglers used to keep such information to themselves. Today in our technology driven world, you can just look on the Internet. Once secret information is now freely shared between anglers on barbel fishing web sites. This has created a need for bigger car parks.

Anglers learn from other anglers. When a big fish is caught from a swim, other anglers will start fishing there, hoping for the same success. I tend to fish between these well-worn swims, as the biggest barbel view them with suspicion. A lot of my fish come from areas far enough away from the hotspots to evade capture, but close enough to capitalize on any discarded bait. If a barbel can be located away from the well-known swims it becomes much easier to catch. The biggest barbel will often take my bait within minutes of it being introduced, as it does not associate the area of the river with danger.

When trying to get to grips with a new fishery, I don't take my fishing tackle with me, thus eliminating any temptation to fish for smaller barbel. This then allows me to concentrate on finding the bigger fish. Stealth is important when approaching the riverbank, as you do not want to scare off any fish. Your choice of clothing should blend in with the surrounding vegetation, so keep low and tread carefully. Rather

than list things to look for I think it would be better to recount some of my experiences that are directly related to observation and location.

BRISTOL AVON SHADOWS

I was walking the banks of the Bristol Avon looking into the river, when I came across what looked like a grey patch of silt. Now I don't know what drew me to this, as there is a lot of silt in the Avon, particularly in the margins. This grey patch was right in the middle of the river and looked out of place against the caramel-coloured background of the riverbed. As my eyesight adjusted to the murkiness, I started to notice movement and shapes. This was no silt patch; it was a solid writhing mass

A 12lb Bristol Avon Shadow.

of barbel. There were fins and tails everywhere. I counted fifteen barbel in all, huddled together, flank to flank and three of them looked very good doubles.

This shoal of barbel grouped together looked so insignificant that they had been overlooked by passing anglers in their hurry to get to the well-known swims. I went on to catch many barbel from this spot, including a 13-pounder, a monster for the Bristol Avon.

Why were they there, as there was plenty of cover nearby? It didn't make any sense to me, a huge shoal of barbel in the middle of nowhere. I had to find out why so I put on some chest waders and went into the river to investigate.

The first thing that I found was that the water was much deeper than I expected. I thought it was only about two feet deep, but it was closer to four. As I waded downstream to the area where the fish were, I noticed what looked like a decaying reed-bed. On closer inspection it turned out to be an old submerged shopping trolley, half buried in the riverbed and covered in sludge and weed. The barbel were lying some five feet downstream of the trolley, in a slight depression in the riverbed that had been hollowed out by the flow as it diverted over the trolley.

I suspected that the barbel had been attracted there by the cover of the shopping trolley. After years of observation I now know that I was wrong in that conclusion. While the trolley did offer limited cover, the fish were there because of the depression. (Although I soon found out to my cost, that shopping trolleys are great bolt-holes for hooked fish.) In my view, depressed areas are the most reliable places to locate barbel on the river. They can range from very deep holes, typically on the bend of a river, to little scrapes, no more than a few inches deeper than the surrounding riverbed. If you can find a depression, no

matter how small, that also has some cover, then you are on to a winner.

PATROL ROUTES

After years of observation, I have concluded that our fisheries are made up of a network of patrol routes. The more time that you spend looking into rivers, the more apparent these become. If you watch barbel as they commute from swim to swim, you will see that they go back and forth, following exactly the same route. The patrol routes are not just confined to barbel, it is my belief that they are used by all river species. The patrol routes are not always the most direct way for the fish to travel, if anything, it is the opposite. Patrol routes are made up of intricate depth changes that go unnoticed by the angler. These troughs and gullies normally take in the best available cover and weave a complex path around the river. To best explain how knowledge of these routes can assist your angling, I will tell you about a capture that I made from a well-worn patrol route.

I was lying down on a high bank, looking at some fish that were in a deep bend on the Great Ouse. On the other bank, an angler was maggot fishing some forty yards upstream. He was fishing a very popular swim and was not aware of the large group of fish downstream. As I watched, a chub swam out of the bend along a line of underwater cabbage on the far bank; it then cut across the river to my bank, passing right underneath me. On my side of the river some of the bank had caved in, depositing a couple of rocks onto the riverbed. The chub approached the rocks and swam between them, when it would have been far easier just to bypass them. The chub then changed sides of the river and swam through a tiny gap in a weed bed and entered the angler's swim where it picked up a mouthful of maggots. The chub then returned to the bend following the exact same route. After a while two barbel repeated precisely the same journey, followed by a large bream and another barbel.

The following day I returned to the high bank with my fishing gear, as one of the barbel looked massive. My approach was to bait with maggots in exactly the same place as the angler had previously. I then waited and watched as barbel after barbel made their way up to the baited area, each taking the same predictable route. Along the cabbage, tight to my bank, through the rocks and into the weed. Eventually the biggest fish in the shoal followed the route upstream to the baited area. As the fish disappeared through the weed bed, I gently lowered a hair-rigged half boilie between

the two rocks. The big barbel started its route back; I was filled with anticipation as it slowly approached the rocks. As the barbel became aware of the boilie it slowed to a stop, giving it a long look. Then it just swam straight over to the bait and picked it up. After a long fight I netted a magnificent fish of over 15lb and was more than happy.

So why didn't I choose to fish the noted swim as I had baited it with maggots? On this stretch the barbel have become very wary when feeding in swims as they associate the areas with danger. Finding a hook-bait between the rocks was probably the last thing the barbel expected. If I had tried to put fishing tackle over the bed of maggots, it is very likely that I would have spooked the fish. I decided to use a boilie hook-bait because there were a lot of small

Guy Robb with a lovely 15lb barbel caught off the 'rocks' on the Great Ouse.

roach and dace around. To use maggots on the hook in this situation would result in one of the small fish hooking itself, which would alarm the barbel. By fishing on the patrol route I was able to catch the biggest barbel by selection. This would not be possible if I had fished in the baited area, as the swim contained many feeding fish. I could not have controlled which one picked up my hook-bait.

Let's take a more detailed look at this patrol route and how the fish make use of cover and depressions. The line of cabbages at the start of the route, were growing at the bottom of a riverbed shelf, here the water was two feet deeper than anywhere else in that section. At the end of the line of cabbages the riverbed started to shallow up. When faced with this open, shallow water the fish diverted across the river to my bank. On inspection, I found the depth to be ten inches more than on the rest of the shallows. The fish then swam to the rocks and took the most awkward route through the middle. Again the water was slightly deeper between the rocks, than it was around them.

This pattern of behaviour has been repeated on every river where I have been able to see barbel. The fish definitely seek out the deeper channels when moving about. Maybe the fish think they are less visible to predators. Once you have built up a good picture of these patrol routes on your own fishery, you will be able to catch fish in the most unlikely looking areas. This knowledge will give you a great advantage in the winter when the water may be high and coloured as those gouged out patrol routes will still be there. You should be able to put your bait in exactly the right place.

Knowledge of patrol routes has taught me never to fish for barbel where they are shoaled up. If you fish where they are shoaled and you catch one, you will spook the rest making another capture unlikely. If you bait an area several yards upstream of the shoal, you can pick the fish off one by one, as they make their way to the food. With care it may be possible to catch the whole shoal.

Well that about covers patrol routes, I hope the example I have given has helped explain them, as knowledge of these routes on your fishery can make a massive difference to your catch rate.

FEEDING PATCHES

You are never too old to learn something new about fish location. This was certainly the case when I started fishing a long and featureless stretch of the Great Ouse. It held a very small population of fish, but some of its residents were monsters. Also it had the advantage of being relatively unknown to other anglers (well that was before the word got around). Finding the fish on this section was frustrating and I was very close to giving up. After many weeks of observation, I hadn't seen a single barbel. I had even fished all the likely looking swims during the day and the night, only catching the occasional chub.

This fishery was a long drive away for me, involving daily traffic jams on the M1 motorway. Things did not improve when I reached the river. To get to the stretch you had to walk about a mile through the muddiest cow fields imaginable. In some parts of the field the mud would come up to your knees. On two occasions I ended up face down in the mud, although it was more dung than mud. I arrived at the riverbank, totally exhausted.

On this particular day I had decided to take a different route across the fields hoping that it would be quicker and easier on my legs. This detour brought me to a different part of the river, which I had previously dismissed as it appeared very shallow and covered in silt and algae. As I stood there, catching my breath after the long trek and while vowing to lose weight, I noticed something interesting in the river – two tea-plate-sized areas of clean golden gravel that stood out against the murky brown of the riverbed.

My first thoughts were that swans had made them, as they foraged around on the bottom, ripping up weed. However, I also thought that feeding fish might have created these patches. With this in mind, I threw out a handful of boilies in the direction of the gravel and made the decision to come back and fish the area after dark.

I returned and fished for an hour or so, but as I didn't get a bite, I decided to pack up. If I am honest I did not expect the swim to produce anyway as it was not what you would call a typical barbel swim. On leaving the swim I threw in my left-over bait and went home.

The following day I went back to the river, as I do hate to be beaten by a fishery. I disregarded the gravel patches from yesterday and just went about fishing my normal swims. After a while and no bites, I decided to go for a walk to see if I could spot any barbel. This took me past the gravel patches, so I decided to take a look at them. I was amazed to see that the gravel patches had grown in size and number, from two to five. I still couldn't be sure of the cause but had to find out. Swans may have seen the discarded bait and made the patches as they picked them up from the riverbed.

I decided to heavily bait up the swim after dark to ensure that the swans couldn't see it and made sure that I was back on the river at first light. If the bait had been eaten, I would know that the fish had eaten it and not the swans.

I arrived back at the swim the very next day just before sunrise. I was more than pleased to find that the bait had all gone

A magnificent 14lb 10oz barbel caught by Guy, after a terrific fight, in gravel feeding patches on the Great Ouse.

and the five small gravel patches had all joined together to form one big area. Now unless the swans had developed night-vision glasses, feeding fish had caused this transformation. Given the lack of cover in this area I thought it was more likely that I would catch these fish at night and was excited about fishing that evening.

I crept quietly into the swim an hour after darkness fell and gently flicked out a hair-rigged boilie (that I had smeared in the same flavoured paste). I let this settle for a while, conscious of the fact that I did not wish to cause too much disturbance in the shallow water. I threw some crumbled boilies around the hook-bait as a further attraction to the fish.

Within seconds of these free offerings hitting the water, I heard an almighty splash some fifty yards downstream. Suddenly there was a large pull on the rod tip and then nothing at all. Was it a line bite? Before I had time to think the rod flew out of the rest, as the butt passed my eyes I managed to grab hold of it. The fight was fantastic, easily the best I had ever had from a barbel. Many times I felt that the fish was going to wrench the rod out of my hands. At 14lb 10oz it was a magnificent first barbel from a new venue.

The moral of this story is that if I had not changed my route to the river and stopped for a breather, I would never have noticed the swim or caught the fish. It taught me to observe the river more carefully and note any unusual features, regardless of how insignificant they may first appear.

RECAPTURED FISH AND CLEARWATER

Clear-water fishing is a great passion of mine. It gives me the opportunity to see how large barbel react to my fishing approach. When the river is clear you must get everything right in terms of tackle and bait. Just remember, if the tackle in the water is clearly seen by you it will also be visible to the fish. Fishing for big barbel in clear water can be frustrating. It is surprising how difficult these fish are to catch as they constantly adapt their behaviour to avoid being hooked.

The biggest barbel are at least 15 years old and have been caught and returned to the river many times. Just think how many recaptures that could be in their life span? In recent years, they have come under mounting pressure from ambitious specimen hunters, who have used the latest innovations in bait and tackle to devastating effect. This has made some of the most targeted fish change their behaviour when feeding.

Nowhere in the country is this more apparent than at the Adams Mill fishery on the Great Ouse. Adams Mill has a small population of large barbel that it shares with its adjoining fishery (thirty barbel over a 2-mile stretch of river). The average size of the fish is now in excess of 14lb. Anglers from all over the country are drawn to the fishery in an attempt to catch one of the six potential record-breaking barbel known to inhabit the stretch. All of the biggest fish have been given pet names because when fish of that size are constantly recaptured, they become well known to the regular anglers. For example, one of the barbel has a long black mark under its eye and is nicknamed Teardrop. Another fish is called Traveller, because it moves between Adams Mill and its neighbouring stretch, and seldom turns up in the same swim twice.

The Adams Mill fish adapt their behaviour almost on a yearly basis, always managing to find a new trick to baffle the angler. I find that a tactic that has been successful one season may not work at all the next. Sometimes there can be up to six massive barbel in a swim, eating free offerings but rarely taking a hook-bait. This can go on for several weeks before a fish is finally caught. Disgruntled anglers turn the air blue as they leave the fishery after yet another blank session.

As I mentioned earlier, most of our rivers are currently going through a decrease in barbel population, resulting in much bigger fish. After all, who would have thought there would ever be 17lb barbel in the river Kennet? Unbelievably, many rivers now have fish in excess of 15lb. These rivers are now coming under increased angling pressure just like Adams Mill. Big fish from these other rivers are already getting recaptured on a regular basis. What happens on the Mill today may happen on your fishery tomorrow.

Even in the clearest water there are various things that can be done to outwit the fish. You could go to any barbel river and see anglers using the same methods as each other and in the same predictable way (static ledgering over a bed of bait). Obviously, after a time the barbel learn what to avoid. Anglers can get stuck in a rut, preferring to stick their heads in the sand with their unfruitful pattern of fishing, rather than embracing change. The message is 'try something different'. If everyone on your stretch fishes with round boilies, use square ones. If no one uses hemp anymore, then buy a sack of it. Try float fishing instead of ledgering. I can't remember when I last saw a barbel angler float fish. These are very simple changes that you can make to improve your catch rate.

It may be a good idea to do all your experimenting with baits and tackle on rivers with large numbers of small barbel. Big fish waters are not the best places to fish if you are unsure of your clear-water tactics. Remember, usually there are not many fish and bites are rare, even when you present your bait perfectly. Once you have perfected your technique you can take on the big fish waters. If you know your approach is right you will fish harder and longer with confidence.

Much of my clear-water fishing is done at close range and there are good reasons for this. A lot of anglers tend to tip their unwanted bait into the margins, which is then eaten by the barbel. The fish soon become accustomed to finding this regular food source that they can eat without fear of being caught, as it is never associated with fishing tackle. If you study how other anglers fish, you will see that they are inclined to cast roughly into the same area of a swim. After a while, the barbel treat the area with extreme caution and become wary of feeding. This is when margin fishing really comes into its own.

When I am margin fishing, I like to move stealthily into a swim, utilizing the natural cover available. I lower a baited hook into six inches of water, right up against the riverbank. In the past I have watched barbel swim over from the other side of the river and pick my bait up without hesitation. Margin fishing allows me to place my bait in exactly the right place without the need to cast. This is important as big barbel do not like the sound of a noisy splash – one clumsy cast and your chance has gone.

MONSTER OF THE MILL

The biggest barbel in the country is nicknamed The Pope and is one of the hardest fish to catch in clear water. It lives on Adams Mill and at the time of writing remarkably has not been caught for two seasons. During the summer this fish can be seen regularly in anglers' swims and is estimated at over 20lb. Most of the time it just swims about, with no intention of feeding. Sometimes it appears agitated when tackle is in the swim. It will go over to the hook-bait and hit it with its tail, as if to try to knock it out of the water. Occasionally, it does respond to small baits, choosing to eat only the free offerings and not the hook-bait. One of the many clever tricks that it does to prevent capture, is to feed only when other barbel are in the swim.

Incredibly, it uses one of the other barbel to test whether or not a bait is connected to fishing tackle. It closely follows the other barbel with its nose to the other's tail while building up speed toward the bed of bait. The leading fish disturbs the baits by positioning itself directly above them, twisting over and over in a sideways rolling action (common behaviour for most barbel). This causes some of the bait to rise up off the riverbed, which the other fish quickly eats before it has time to settle back onto the bottom. Bait that remains on the bottom is ignored; this would include a hook-bait as the weight of the hook keeps it pinned to the riverbed.

This feeding pattern would be repeated several times. Eventually the leading barbel would stop its excited rolling and settle down to feed normally. When this happens the other larger fish loses interest in feeding and just goes back to swimming about. By adopting this strange feeding pattern, the big barbel can be sure, that all the bait that it eats is safe.

THE WAY TO CATCH THE MONSTER

A few anglers have observed this peculiar feeding pattern and have adapted their rigs accordingly in order to catch this fish. They made their hook-bait look and act like one of the free offerings. Buoyant material was added to the end rigs to compensate for the weight of the hook. This is called bait balancing. I automatically do this nowadays because more and more barbel are becoming wary around fishing tackle.

Various buoyancy materials can be used to suit different baits. I add a little slither of white rig foam to my hook when using maggots as this removes weight from the hook and emulates a maggot. A snowman rig is used when boilie fishing. This consists of two mini-boilies on a hair. One boilie is made from a pop-up mix (microwave) and the other from a standard mix (boil). The pop-up boilie is attached to the hair at the furthest point away from the hook. When submerged the buoyancy of the mix makes this rig stand up on the riverbed and looks similar to a snowman.

Making rigs like the two above will require a bit of time and effort, but will be worthwhile in the end. The most successful big fish anglers whom I know update and change their rigs to stay ahead of the fish and other anglers. You can learn a lot by experimenting with your own ideas and materials. For instance, try emptying some bait into a bath full of water (when your wife is out). Agitate the water above the sunken bait to mirror the disturbance made by a feeding barbel. Look to see how the bait reacts in the water and then add your standard unbalanced baited hook-rig. You should see a difference in movement between the loose baits and the ones on your hook. To rectify the situation you can try adding bits of polystyrene, cork, foam or pop-up mix until you have achieved a balanced hook-bait. Alternatively, it is now possible to buy buoyant imitation baits like maggots and pellets that can be added to a genuine hook-bait to fool even the smartest barbel. When finished the baited hook should only just sink and become dislodged from the bottom more easily than the loose bait. I never use a hook bigger than a size 8 as I like to keep the hook weight to the minimum for balancing. It is a good idea to buy a range of different coloured marker pens so that you can match the buoyant material to your bait.

WISING UP TO HAIR-RIGS

Barbel fishing is developing in much the same way that carp fishing did twenty years ago. Although traditional baits like maggots, meat and corn are still widely used, there has been an upsurge in the use of pellets and boilies. These baits are harder in consistency and are not suitable for mounting directly on to a hook, which has led to the more common use of the hair-rig (standard hair-rig – ¾in hair with a ½in bait). While still effective at catching barbel, it's becoming apparent that the fish are wising up to its use. I have seen big barbel picking up anglers hair-rigged baits in their mouths and spitting them out again without the angler even knowing.

Through my own observations, I would say that pressured barbel learn how to deal with hair-rigs quicker than carp. We must remember that the hair-rig isn't any different from other methods used and if flogged to death will lose its effectiveness. Carp anglers have had decades of experience with both hair-rigs and recaptured fish. They have developed a number of different types of hair-rig to keep the fish guessing. I recommend that you purchase a good carp fishing rig book that should help you develop effective rigs suitable for your barbel fishing.

I first became aware that heavily pursued barbel were adapting the way they picked up hair-rigs, while watching some barbel feed in a fellow angler's swim. He was complaining that although he had gone to great lengths to disguise himself and his tackle, he still wasn't getting a bite. I was intrigued and decided to move to a better vantage point. I climbed onto the branches of an overhanging tree on the bank opposite his swim. This gave me a clearer view of the fish and of the angler's bait (a hair-rigged boilie).

I was astounded to see that every single fish in that swim had picked up and indeed dropped his hook-bait. Informing the angler of my sightings, he replied that he had noticed that his quiver tip had only registered a few faint little taps. In fact this had been happening to him all day, which he had disregarded as the activity of minnows. He had logically expected a barbel to hook itself, when it picked up the hair-rig. I then went into detail with him and explained that on closer inspection the barbel were just clamping half of the boilie between their lips, making sure that the attached hook stayed on the outside of their mouths. They would then slowly back away, still holding the end of the boilie and when they felt the resistance of the rod tip, they would drop the bait.

I have chatted with fellow anglers who also fish in popular stretches of river up and down the country about the sneaky behaviour of barbel when in contact with hair-rigs. Most of them have experienced the same faint tapping on their rod tips, especially at night. Theoretically there could be more taps at night because as the barbel cannot see the bait they rely more on their mouths to test for any resistance from tackle. The more we talked, the more it became apparent that they were all using standard hair-rigs in conjunction with running leads. I let them know about the last time I used this rig on a big fish water when I watched a massive barbel pick up my hair-rigged boilie (12mm) and swim off, with the hook clearly dangling from its mouth. The rod tip was pulled more than 2ft by the barbel before it dropped the bait.

HAIR-RIG FOR CAGEY BARBEL

If I encounter the problems discussed above I now know that in order to catch the barbel I must change to a heavy fixed lead rig that incorporates a small hook. I have caught a lot of fish using this rig and always have a couple tied up in my rig pouch just in case. The rig consists of a very heavy lead (4oz minimum) and a small hook (size 10 maximum). I use a broken piece of boilie for the bait because it needs to be tiny (5mm approximately). The lead must be fixed to the line by a safety clip to ensure the quick release of the lead in the event of a fish becoming tethered. Make sure that the hook length is between 4in and 6in long and that the hair is kept extremely short. When this rig is finished, the tiny piece of bait should sit tightly against the shank of the hook.

As the fish takes the bait, it commits itself to the hook automatically, because the barbel has difficulty picking up such a small offering between its lips. When the bait enters its mouth the hook is set straight away by the heavy lead and that is why the rig is so effective. It is important to use a lead of at least 4oz as a lighter one will not drive home the hook into the barbel's lip. As the fish is hooked, the slight rod tip movements will cease and will become a violent lunge as the fish bolts away.

Beware, there is a drawback to this rig and it should only be used when you are getting cagey bites on your standard set-up. The small hook-rig has a poor pull-out rate and my fingers are usually crossed hoping and praying that it does not fall out while playing the fish. The reason it can fall out is because the heavy lead hangs down from the fish's mouth and can pull the hook loose. However, give it a try as it may make a big difference to your catch rate.

THINKING DIFFERENTLY

Let's look at a tactic that I generally apply when faced with wary barbel that can be used to great effect on any clear-running barbel water. This method has been formulated in response to findings from hours of observation. The correct placement of bait is key to my success. For example, at Adams Mill the barbel are reluctant to pick up bait from the gravel riverbed because they have been caught there many times before. However, when I place my bait on top of something else (weed, underwater cabbage, rocks, old tin can) they do not hesitate to eat it.

I made a great capture from an unlikely spot on Adams Mill after chatting to a couple of local anglers there. They told me that part of the bank had collapsed into the river depositing a mound of clay and rubble. They also said, that a huge barbel had been spotted lying just behind the mound that other anglers had tried unsuccessfully to catch. So I made my way down to that part of the river where I soon found the barbel nestling behind a huge lump of clay. The fish was just lying on the bottom, almost lifeless but occasionally moved its fins to hold position. I could see that the bank-side grass was still attached to the top of the mound that was submerged in 3ft of water with only about 1ft between the top of the mound and the waterline.

Hoping to lure the barbel out from behind the mound, I decided to fish just upstream from it. I placed a tiny boilie hook-bait gently onto the riverbed then crumbled up some broken boilies and trickled them in around it and settled down to watch. After a few minutes, the barbel backed out from behind the mound and made its way up to the bait. It swam around the baited area for a short while, and then returned to its original position. I sat there for a further hour and so did the barbel, not stirring once.

It was then that I remembered a remarkable capture that I had made at Kings Weir on the river Lea. The swims at Kings Weir were pegged and the resident fish were used to being caught from those areas. I found that doing something different often resulted in a capture. On one occasion, I had caught a couple of barbel from the top of a submerged boulder that had once formed part of the old weir pool wall. These fish had resisted all attempts to catch them while I had my hook-bait on the riverbed, but as soon as I put my bait onto the rock they took it straight away. I had a similar experience when fishing the Royalty on the Hampshire Avon, this time a barbel picked up the hook-bait from a sunken piece of corrugated tin that had become wedged into the riverbed. The same barbel would not touch the bait, when it was placed on the gravel.

With these successful captures in mind, I decided to try the same tactic with this monster. So I lowered my bait into the water about twenty feet upstream of the barbel and the clay mound. Then while keeping low I got myself into position directly above the fish and the collapsed bank. I then proceeded to reel in the tackle, slowly, so that I could see the hook-bait coming down mid-river toward the rod tip. When the bait reached the clay mound, I stopped reeling in and lowered the rod tip. This enabled the hook-bait to gently settle on top of the clay mound, without the tackle disturbing the water.

The barbel may have become alarmed if I had tried to place the hook-bait directly on top of the clay mound, as essentially, it was only two feet above its head. I could watch to see if there was any reaction from the huge barbel, now that the bait was in the right position. After about ten minutes, the barbel backed itself out from behind the rubble and headed upstream, sensing that there was food about. Searching for the food, the fish swam up and down the river, in the vicinity of the clay mound several times, still unaware of where the bait actually was. By this time I could see that the fish was getting agitated and it began pushing its head against the rubble in an aggressive manner.

All of a sudden the barbel rose up in the water, and swam back and forth across the top of the baited hook. It was fantastic to see this large barbel at such a close range. Its massive tail broke the surface of the water as the barbel dipped its head down over the bait. The fish was hooked. After a long battle, a marvellous looking 15lb barbel was on the bank.

USING THE RIGHT TACKLE

Rods

Acquiring knowledge of big barbel behaviour and their preferences will enhance your catch rate dramatically. However, to get the best results you must use a suitable rod in conjunction with well-thought-out tackle. In a lot of my old fishing books it was suggested that a test curve of 1¼lb was ideal for barbel fishing. Generally, I think this is good advice for medium-sized barbel (5lb–9lb) and not for the larger sized specimens that we catch today. In the space of a few years, the barbel record has jumped from 14lb to over 20lb. Given that many fisheries now have barbel weighing 15lb and more, I feel that it is necessary to use a rod with a test curve of at least 1 1.2 lb and sometimes 1.10lb (floodwater and snag-filled rivers). I do not rely solely on the manufacturer's stated test curves, as no two rods are the same and I suggest that you try them out. I have tried some stated 1¼lb test curve rods that felt a lot stiffer than some 2lb ones.

My ideal rod is between 11ft and 12ft and must have a nice progressive action. It must be able to deliver a great deal of power, when required. The extra power should be in the 18in of rod directly above the butt. My preference is a two-piece rod as I find that the three-piece ones have too many flat spots that can affect the rod's action. I have developed my own rod to suit these requirements with the addition of a separate top section with three interchangeable quiver tips. The Guy Robb All River Rod can be purchased directly from me by telephoning 07743 139801.

When buying a barbel rod, get the shopkeeper to hold the rod tip down to the floor while you lift the butt end up slowly. You are looking for a perfect arc, with little or no flat spots. Then with the shopkeeper still holding the tip down, lift the rod up as hard as you can which should enable you to feel the power just above the butt. Try and lift the shopkeeper off the floor. If the rod keeps bending all the way down to the butt, it is too soft or if the rod bends easily on the top section, but looks like a broomstick below the joint, it is too stiff. It is important not to use a rod that is too stiff as it can cause the hook to pull out from the fish's mouth during the fight.

If the rod snaps don't buy it; the shopkeeper may moan but better it breaks in the shop than on a 16lb barbel. The rod that you eventually purchase should act like a powerful but forgiving shock absorber, capable of wearing out the biggest barbel.

Rigs and Line

My selections of rigs and line are chosen mainly because they blend in with the riverbed and I have tried many different ones to find the most suitable for clearwater fishing. Unfortunately, many products in the tackle shops that may look good on the shelves have no practical use when submerged in the water, as the fish can see them easily plus the fact that some are too fragile for the larger fish. However, some good items of tackle can be found in the carp section of the shop as carp anglers have already recognized the need for this type of tackle. It is possible to make your tackle virtually invisible to a barbel and for it still to be strong enough to land it.

I use Big Game clear 10lb line when fishing in a clear river as I find it both ultra-reliable and cost-effective. This abrasive resistant line has never let me down and is much less visible in the water than any other coloured line that I have used. Some anglers favour braid or coloured lines but as an experiment, try putting some clear line, over the edge of a pint glass, alongside coloured line and braid. You will see for yourself, when you fill the glass with water and hold it up to the light, why I use the clear line.

Backleading

Although I use clear line, I still prefer to sink the mainline to the riverbed whenever possible, removing it totally from the fish's sight. I do this with a running backlead that I attach three feet up the mainline away from the hook-rig. A small-drilled bullet lead is used, with the size being dependent on the river flow (fast flows need heavier back leads). This backlead is held in place with a power gum stop knot. It is important that your backlead is of adequate weight, or you may end up with a drilled bullet lead flapping about in the water right above the barbel's head

I also use backleads to remove the sound of line vibration that is caused by the river flow hitting the mainline. My final use of backleads is to prevent line bites, which must be avoided when fishing for big barbel. The larger fish have been caught before and spook easily around fishing tackle.

Coated Leads and Accessories

When clear-water fishing, it is far better to use the green/brown-coated leads rather than the uncoated shiny ones that most people use. This is because, ideally, the leads should blend into the background of the riverbed. I used to use the shiny leads but on sunny days I noticed that the lead glistened in the clear water, which obviously alarmed the fish. It is now possible to buy stone ledger weights, which takes camouflage in clear water one step further or you can try making your own. (Glue some dried silt onto a standard lead.)

When using accessories like rubber connectors or tubing, do avoid using the black ones, as they do not blend into the background I find the green ones much better. You may need to consider camouflaging your swivels with dried silt as they also glisten in clear water just like the uncoated leads.

There are two hook link materials that I use in clear water. For my standard rig I use 12lb Drennan micro-braid that is a sandy-brown colour and does seem to blend in well with the riverbed. I wrap a tiny piece of wire in the middle of my hook link, which helps to pin it to the riverbed, as braid tends to float. My other favoured hook link is 8lb Drennan fly leader. I find this hook link material virtually invisible in clear water and it has helped me to land some big fish. This material can be fragile, so it is best to replace the hook link after catching a fish.

Hooks
Until quite recently most barbel baits were mounted directly onto the hook itself. The subject of hook selection did not warrant much serious attention. A hook was deemed suitable as long as it didn't bend while playing and landing a fish. The angler striking at a bite caused the hook to pull upwards and into the fish's top lip, creating a firm hook hold.

Hair-rigs now dominate the big barbel scene. Your choice of hook is vital when using this type of rig because of the way the fish is hooked. How does a barbel get hooked on a hair-rig as opposed to the traditional method that I have already mentioned? With a hair-rig, a barbel will pick up the bait and automatically take the bare hook into its mouth. The hook hangs below the bait and when the barbel is aware of the hook in its mouth, it panics and bolts away. This action causes the hook to pull into its lower lip, which can be a drawback as the hook hold on a barbel's lower lip is not as secure as it would be in its top lip. In order to reduce the chances of the hook pulling out while playing a fish, it is important to use the correct hook pattern.

A hook with an inturned eye is my choice when hair-rigging. When pressure is applied to this hook, via the rod and line, the inturned eye design helps bury the hook point, deeper into the fish's lip. I never use a hook with an outturned eye as it has the opposite effect and pulls out far too easily.

Another factor to take into consideration, when choosing a hook for hair-rigging in clear water, is the visibility of the hook itself. When a barbel approaches your bait it may be able to see your hook lying next to the bait. After experimentation in the margins of the river, I concluded that silver hooks are by far the best option as the black and gold ones were too visible. My favourites at the moment are Frank Warwick Insizzors and Kevin Nash Fangs that are both silver and inturned.

OTHER CLEAR-WATER TACKLE TRICKS

A lot of my fishing is done, in very small gaps in the weed and close to the riverbank because the barbel feed comfortably in these areas as they have plenty of cover. Sometimes, these gaps are no more than a few inches wide. It is difficult to present your tackle properly and the biggest problem to overcome is the visibility of the mainline, as there is not enough room to use a backlead. The line must be hidden as a barbel is bound to see it, or worse still bump into it.

I disguise the line, to look like a strand of weed by threading two feet of green rig tubing over it. It is then connected to my lead by means of a Korda lead clip and rubber. I fish this set-up with my line quite slack, making the rig tubing appear limp in the water. When this is completed it fools the barbel into thinking that it is just a strand of weed. This stops the fish being alarmed if it should bump against the tubing as it feels nothing like a tight fishing line. I have caught dozens of very big fish on this rig despite its bizarre appearance.

Alternatively, when I fish near reedbeds, I slit a reed with a knife and bury the line within it, closing the whole thing securely with four green garden ties. I slide the reed down until it reaches the lead. I use a very heavy lead (5oz), as the reed can be easily dislodged by the flow. I use a 4in hook length and once finished, this can be placed amongst other reeds without detection. Getting a bite on this rig is an absolute delight, as I watch the 3ft reed tear off downstream.

VERY COLD WATER

It can be quite a challenge to fish for barbel when there is frost on the ground and the margins of the river are frozen. Most of the time barbel fishing under these conditions is not worth the effort. In very cold water the barbel spends most of its time in a semi-dormant state. Its requirement for food is greatly reduced due to a slow-down in the barbel's metabolic rate. If the river is freezing cold and running clear, the barbel may only feed for ten minutes in a 24-hour period.

When I was more of a general barbel angler, fishing highly populated stretches of river, I used to persevere in these cold conditions and was just glad to catch a barbel of any size. Today, I fish mainly for large barbel and find these very cold conditions a waste of time as big-targeted barbel are hard enough to catch when they are hungry and almost impossible when they are not. The main reason that I don't persevere in these conditions is because the river becomes over-baited due to large numbers of anglers trying to catch a big fish, regardless of water temperature. The scenario could be as follows on any given day in freezing cold conditions:

20 barbel × 2 boilies = 40 baits needed to satisfy fish population.

10 anglers × 30 boilies = 300 boilies chucked into the river.

Conclusion: 260 boilies in excess of the barbel's requirements means that no one catches that day.

To gain any success in these conditions it is far better just to use a few maggots, with half a pint being plenty for a session. When

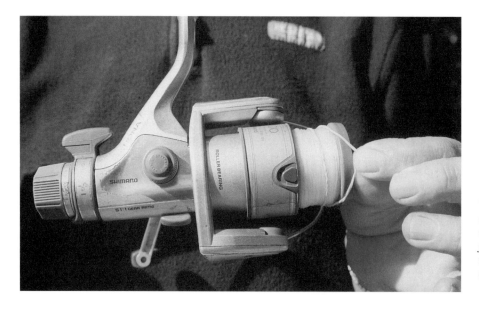

To help achieve accurate casting when using a feeder, place a rubber band on the reel spool to 'stop' the line.

fishing bigger rivers like the Severn or the Thames use a small swim-feeder full of maggots and only cast out every thirty minutes. It is vital to cast accurately when fishing with a swim-feeder in cold water, as it is important not to spread the feed all over the river; barbel will not waste energy hunting for the food. One of the easiest ways to guarantee accurate casting is to cast out to the desired spot and then simply place a rubber band over your reel spool. When you reel in and cast out again the line will be stopped by the rubber band, making sure the feeder lands in the same place time after time.

IDEAL WINTER CONDITIONS

In the winter, I prefer to wait for some warm, westerly rain to arrive, before I seriously think about barbel fishing. When the river temperature rises and some extra coloured water comes into the river, the barbel will eat voraciously. However, if the river is coloured due to snow melt, or if a lot of road salt has been washed into the river, the fish are less likely to feed as the snowmelt makes the water colder and the road salt can deoxygenate the water. When the water level is high and coloured, it is possible to use less refined tackle, as the barbel cannot see so well.

When hair-rigging in high, coloured water, I find braided hook links are prone to constant tangling, as a result of the increased river flow. In these conditions, I use an anti-tangle product called Snakeskin that has a stiff plastic coating. It is designed so that you can strip away some of the outer coating that reveals a very soft but strong white inner material; this gives flexibility around the hook, a requirement when hair-rigging. I reveal ½in of inner material, directly above the hook. The hair can be made out of the same soft inner material by using a knotless knot. However, this material can be awkward to manipulate as it is made up of individual fibres. I make mine separately, using a standard braid that I whip around the hook. Snakeskin is highly visible and therefore only suitable for coloured-water conditions.

Highly coloured water in the winter is often associated with flooding and can deter anglers from their sport. However, floodwater can be very productive as it is usually warmer water – a result of the warmer rain being swept in on westerly winds. I wait until the initial floodwater has swept through the river, taking all the debris with it (whole trees, dead cows, and so on). Then I fish using very heavy sea leads (6oz), the dimpled watch leads are the best as they grip the river-bed, despite the increased volume of water.

The barbel are not hard to catch, they are just hard to locate in these conditions. It is quite common to find all of the barbel on the stretch, shoaled up in a few areas. The fish like to be more comfortable and rest from the raging river flow. The choice of high-water swim will be made much easier, if likely areas are spotted when the river is running clear. If the barbel patrol routes have been noted in the summer, you should be able to present the bait in exactly the right spot, regardless of the volume of water. If faced with a stretch of water that is unfamiliar, seek out the slower, steadier looking swims. A lot of the time, the fish are close to their summer swims and may only have moved a few yards away. In the summer, barbel can be found on the outside of a bend but in high winter water, the same fish may have moved across to the slower water on the inside.

Look for calm and flat bits of water. Barbel feed readily in these conditions and by far the most successful way of locating fish in coloured water is to keep on the move.

WINTER METHODS

When fishing a static hair-rig in winter, I lightly bait a number of possible swims with some broken-up boilies and dissolvable pellets. I then leave the spots for about an hour before fishing them. I fish each of the swims for a short time only, unless I get some action, as most bites come within a couple of minutes of casting. Generally, I fish a hair-rigged 10mm boilie with a thin layer of the boilie mix paste wrapped around it. Paste is used in this way in winter because it leaks more flavour than a boilie in cold water. Also, if all of the paste dissolves off or gets nibbled away by small fish, the hair-rigged boilie remains in the water.

In conjunction with this rig, I hang 6in of PVA string on the end of the exposed hook. Attached to the PVA are some small broken pieces of boilie and a couple of pea-sized blobs of paste. A little trail of bait is created from the dissolved PVA string that the barbel will follow, all the way up to the hook-bait.

I always fish a few yards upstream from where I have introduced my pre-bait, as I do not want to cast directly above the feeding area of the fish. Once the rig is in place, I crumble up a boilie and trickle it in, just upstream of my hook-bait enticing the fish to move toward my fishing position.

This method has proved to be highly effective for me especially when the river is carrying extra water. If I know the river well and have a good idea where the barbel patrol routes are, then I can dispense with the pre-bait and put the hook-bait in exactly the right place. Although this static

OPPOSITE: To find barbel in coloured water conditions you need to keep moving along the riverbank.

method is productive, it can get boring, so when this happens I rove the stretch, trundling single hook-baits like meat or paste along the riverbed. This allows me to search every nook and cranny of the river for a feeding fish. Ideal winter conditions are peak times for barbel fishing and should be when you fish the hardest. The barbel are at their largest weights and they are also easier to catch. Successful winter fishing is synonymous with reading the weather and river conditions correctly and putting this knowledge to good use.

PROTEIN BAITS, A PERSONAL VIEW

For the modern barbel angler, milk protein powder, trout pellets and highly nutritional value products are the favoured choice of bait. These baits have been adopted from carp fishing and are easily available in all tackle shops. In the past, we used to purchase all of the barbel bait (luncheon meat, sausages, sweetcorn, cheese and bread) from the supermarket. While many barbel anglers see the new-style baits as an opportunity to extend their boundaries in their fishing approach, others see them as a threat to their more traditional methods. I think the modern baits are a welcome addition to good watercraft and perfect presentation skills. I find that if these new baits are used with careful consideration, they can achieve fantastic results and catch many fish but if they are not used correctly, they perform no better than traditional bait.

Designer baits have secretly been used to great effect in barbel angling for decades with many great catches not being reported. The first of the new-style baits to hit the barbel scene was milk protein, mostly made from processed milk

Designer bait.

ingredients such as calcium caseinate, casein and lactalbumin. This bait found its way into barbel angling via a number of knowledgeable carp anglers. The carp anglers knew all about fish nutrition, bait and how to make a perfect recipe that would prove irresistible to barbel.

This information was shared with a small group of good barbel anglers and put to the test. The recipe was kept a closely guarded secret. It became impossible to keep the success of the bait under wraps as the chosen group of barbel anglers started to empty stretches of river that were thought to be difficult to fish. They attracted a lot of criticism from other barbel anglers who resented their catches and

some people said that the use of this bait was classed as cheating. Politics set in and petty resentments were rife amongst the barbel fraternity. The anglers who used the new bait were being rubbished by the non-users, which in some extreme cases sadly led to a few anglers giving up their sport altogether. I personally thought the catches were fantastic and it inspired me to learn more about the new baits.

Looking back at those early successes, I rate the catch made by Dave Williams from the Hampshire Avon as the best of all time. Tackling one of the hardest stretches of the river, he caught all of the big resident fish, in just a couple of days, that is, three fish over 14lb, as well as many 12- and

13lb monsters. This catch deserved more praise than it actually received.

Fortunately, the modern designer baits are now manufactured and are freely available to all anglers. However, some anglers still source their own ingredients, believing that a pure milk protein recipe is far better than any commercial mixes currently on the market. While I must concede that these homemade milk baits are superb, I still think that the skill and determination of the anglers are the main factors contributing to their successful barbel catches. I believed that these baits had no significant advantage over good commercial mixes and decided to experiment extensively in controlled conditions to find out more. My findings were that the fish had no particular preference for either the manufactured or the homemade recipes. In the early years, milk baits were considerably different from other baits available. Now, kilos of similar shop-bought protein baits go into the river looking, smelling and tasting no different from homemade milk bait. While the milk protein levels in a commercial mix may be less than in a homemade one (due to cost) they are close enough to be indistinguishable to barbel. Good commercial mixes contain vitamins and minerals, which is important for the welfare of the fish.

The concentrated milk protein baits take a long time for barbel to digest, especially in cold water. In the winter, be careful not to overfeed the fish as neither you nor anybody else will get a bite for days afterwards. All of my barbel fishing is done using a base mix that is lower in milk protein. It has been formulated to be visually appealing, nutritional, easily digestible and flavoursome, which allows me to fish with a reasonable amount of bait in cold-water conditions without overfeeding.

I have total faith in the range of John Baker baits and these products have helped me to catch many monster-sized barbel including my British record fish. John Baker takes the subject of bait very seriously and only ever uses fresh ingredients in his mixes and does not add any preservatives. To get the best results from these baits you must be willing to adapt their use to your own fishery' requirements. For example, if you feel that the barbel on your stretch have become wary of round-shaped boilies, change the size and shape of them. Small changes can significantly improve your catch rate and remember the importance of presentation and location, as these will help you get the best from your bait.

MAKING THE *UP CLOSE AND PERSONAL* VIDEO

I have always had a real passion for barbel fishing and like to meet other anglers who feel the same. This was certainly the case when I met fellow barbel addict, Stuart Morgan. I was fishing a weir pool on the Bristol Avon when Stuart came up to chat and I could tell straight away that he would be a good laugh to fish with. After that first meeting, we decided to fish together and also experiment with different baits and fishing tactics. Stuart tried out some baits made by John Baker and was regularly catching more barbel than me. After many weeks of this, I was in a huge sulk and requested a meeting between John Baker and myself. The three of us became firm friends, sharing the same passion for barbel fishing and we then all regularly fished together.

We preferred to fish at close range and caught a lot of barbel. This method allowed us to study the fish in greater detail and to actually see the reaction of the fish to the chosen tackle and bait. At the time, Stuart was living close to the banks of the Bristol

Avon and the beauty of this river is that it runs gin-clear during the summer months, making for easier observation. We were able to see groups of fish in obscure places although we did have to kneel in beds of stinging nettles and hang from trees to do so. The more inaccessible the bank side, the more likely we were to find a group of fish.

The early trials of John Baker's barbel mix were first tried on the new-found shoals of fish. Large barbel, some as big as 13lb, were literally eating bait off the riverbank. They were half exposing their bodies out of the water in order to get to the food. We had never seen anything like this before

and thought that other anglers might also like to see it for themselves. So Stuart took his video camera with him the next day to film them eating the bait in this manner. The footage was amazing.

At that stage, there was never any intention to make a video and those early snippets of film remained unseen for years. In those early days, the John Baker barbel bait was still in its developmental stages and we were the only three anglers who were using it. There was no spare time for filming, just time for catching the fish.

Stuart was emptying the Bristol Avon of its barbel population on a daily basis and I had moved on to the Bedfordshire Ouse. It

Filming the barbel video entitled Up Close and Personal. *Guy holds a beautiful 14lb 10oz fish.* (Credit G. Purnell)

was closer to where I lived in Buckinghamshire and I chose a particular stretch of the river that held some of the biggest and most pursued barbel in the country. I wasn't sure if I could get the fish as interested in the new bait as their cousins were, on the Bristol Avon. Once, I had modified my approach to take into account the fishing pressure from other anglers, I started to catch large barbel (14–15lb) on a regular basis. Within a couple of seasons, I had managed to catch every big fish known on that stretch.

In my first season of using the bait, I broke the Ouse river record. I phoned Stuart and asked him to meet me at the river straightaway to witness and verify the 15lb 12oz whopper (The Pope). We both marvelled at the size of this creature, wondering if we would ever see specimens of this weight again.

The following day, I was the one who got a phone call, this time from Stuart who said that he had just broken The Bristol Avon record with another 15-pounder. My first reaction was that he was joking. What were the odds of two river records being exceeded on consecutive days, especially when one of the anglers had just witnessed the other on the previous day. He had indeed caught a whopper. Demand for John's bait increased from other anglers wanting the same success for themselves.

Having tired of fishing the well-known stretch of the Ouse, I decided to try a less known fishery just downstream and the results were even better. The great thing about this fishery was that hardly anybody else fished there, particularly in the winter months. It was an arduously long walk to get there, through some of the muddiest bogs imaginable. I got to know that the composition of the bogs was about 10 per cent soil and 90 per cent cow dung after falling face first in them on several trips. I fished there for a couple of years and got to

know the stretch really well, catching barbel regularly. There were seven or eight fish on the stretch in excess of 15lb. Today, these fish have increased in size and weigh from 17lb to nearly 20lb. Stuart was still catching many doubles out of the Bristol Avon.

On one of our fishing trips together, we decided that it would be fun to try and make a barbel video. We wanted to make a film that concentrated on the barbel behaviour, rather than have a collection of trophy shots. After all, we both enjoyed watching barbel as much as catching them. The idea was to show how barbel reacted to our baits and tactics and we set about getting some underwater footage on the Bristol Avon in three different locations. As a finale to our video we were hoping to catch a 15lb barbel from the quiet stretch of the Ouse and film it. This project was achieved using a hand held video camera, in our spare time.

To look at the finished film would suggest that everything had gone to plan without any hiccups. In reality, there were an awful lot of blunders and swearing outtakes, most of which I still have on tape and may be used to blackmail Stuart with at a later date. While we both knew what we wanted to film, it was a lot harder to get the barbel to participate. It was guaranteed that if we went to the river without the camera, we would catch all day and the barbel might even perform a song and dance act on the riverbank. When we took the camera with us, they were nowhere to be seen. A major problem to contend with was the weather, as we needed blue sky and sunny days. The cloud stopped the required light penetration. Planned weekend filming sometimes produced disappointing blurry shots of fish.

People often say that they enjoyed the scenes of the fish in and under the water and ask how we achieved this. The best

Guy proudly displays his British record barbel that weighed 17lb 6oz 12dr and was caught on the Ouse.

fish-in-the-water scenes took many weeks to get and used up hours of tape. A professional cameraman would have got those shots in no time, but we were complete amateurs, learning as we went. The shots taken above the water were done using both of our cameras (Hi-8 hand-held video cameras) with polarizing filters attached to the lenses. The cameras were mounted onto tripods and the film was left to run. This was especially useful when we wanted fishing scenes, where both of us, and the barbel were needed to be in a shot.

We came up with the idea of filming underwater and Stuart built a construction that looked like a huge triangular upright greenhouse. It stood about 4ft tall and 18in wide. The whole thing was made of glass and held together with sealant. A video camera was going to be contained in this mobile greenhouse and I was to wade out into 3ft of the Bristol Avon, and try to push it down to the bottom of the river-bed for filming. Stuart was then going to wade out with a paving slab and put it on top of the whole apparatus in order to keep it stable and in position.

What a laugh that was. I could not force it down into the water any more than three inches because of the massive amount of air pressure within the huge construction. I pushed down on this monster as hard as I could and in the end it shattered in my hands. Luckily this was a trial run and the camera was not in it. Modifications were needed so we decided that in order to sink the camera, we would have to use a watertight container slightly bigger than the camera itself thus reducing excess air.

We ended up with a piece of opaque plastic pipe with a watertight removable cap on one end and a clear glass panel

sealed into the other. It was not much bigger than the camera but it still required a cradle made from 40lb of lead in order to sink it. Once this had been tested and found to be watertight, we risked Stuart's camera as I refused point blank to use mine. The activated camera and housing unit was lowered into known barbel habitats by means of a long rope and left to record until the end of the tape. Barbel seemed curious and sometimes the fish would go right up to the glass and look inside at the camera. This prompted us to

The record-breaker is returned to the river.

Guy with a lovely Ouse 16-pounder.

place bait down in front of the camera and watch them feed. We even managed to hook a couple, right in front of the lens.

The filming went into the following year and was taking a lot longer than first thought. In the winter of the first season, we went to the Ouse to try and catch a big fish for the video and it was during this period that I caught my British Record barbel. The following season, Stuart returned to the Ouse and broke the record two more times. We were able to get my record fish and Stuart's on camera. By the

end of our filming, we had a bag full of videotape that needed to be edited. The intention was to put together the finished film without outside help. However, it soon became obvious that this was way beyond our capabilities.

That didn't stop us trying. Some of the funniest moments I have ever had on the riverbank came during our attempts to introduce each section of the film by talking directly to the camera. On one occasion, Stuart was introducing a piece, about close-in fishing and explaining how he had carefully baited a swim just behind him where the barbel were feeding well. I could see through the camera lens a large black and white cow on the far bank just behind Stuart's prepared swim and just above a sheer drop. All of a sudden, the cow plunged upside down straight into Stuart's swim and on top of the feeding fish. It then swam up and down several times over his carefully baited swim. As the startled cow tried to get out, it would shoot a jet of water three feet into the air via its nostrils while mooing. Needless to say, that was the end of filming for the day and any more out-takes available for 'you've been framed'. Was this taking milk protein bait too far?

There were many attempts to do serious introductions but nine times out of ten we would just end up in a fit of the giggles and would have to give up. Time drifted by and we were not putting in the time required in order to finish the film. In the early days, we would happily take days off from work at a moment's notice, if we thought that the river conditions were perfect for filming. In the end, we ceased to find the project a pleasure. At this point, John Baker was shown some of the footage and he suggested that we contact Len Gurd a specialist in fishing videos. Len was interested in the project and agreed to edit the video footage and refilm the links. At the time I was glad to see the back of filming. When I look back now, I realize it was one of the most interesting things I have taken part in and certainly one of the funniest.

Ray Walton

Ray was born in Hampstead, London, in 1952 and has been fishing for barbel since the early 1970s. He joined the Barbel Catchers Club in 1982 and contributed a chapter on the Royalty Fishery in Barbel by the Barbel Catchers and Friends (Crowood Press, 1988). He also wrote a chapter in the first edition of Quest For Barbel by Tony Miles and Trefor West (Crowood Press, 1991) and supplied most of the photographs for the book. Ray has also had his photographs published in Understanding Barbel by Fred Couch and a number of other books. He has written barbel articles for various angling magazines over a 25-year period and has worked as a freelance photographer and journalist for the Angler's Mail, Angling Times and Improve Your Coarse Fishing.

In the late 1980s Ray formed the Barbel Study Group, he was a founder member of the Barbel Society established in the mid-1990s and he formed the Barbel Specialist Group in 2001. He has also appeared in videos and on television programmes such as Andy Little's Angling Adventures, Screaming Reels, Take Nobody's Word For It and Tight Lines. Ray has made his own video on the Great Ouse entitled Ousing Barbel. He fishes exclusively for barbel and studies only this species of fish.

This 12lb 8oz fish was attracted by rolling meat. It was one of five barbel that Ray caught in mid-afternon in the House Pool above the rapids on the Royalty Fishery on the Hampshire Avon.

4 It's Only Rock 'n' Roll!

by Ray Walton

REELIN' IN THE YEARS

I started fishing the Royalty Fishery on the Hampshire Avon in the early 1970s when the most productive part of the river was the upper section above the main car park. At the time, the name of the game was to pile in a gallon of maggots or more at the Pipes, in the Parlour, Railway Pool, Boathouse or other known swims. This practice was used to draw in the huge barbel shoals that inhabited the fishery, as much as hemp did in the later years on other rivers. It eventually caused a bit of a rumpus as the barbel moved in from other areas and congregated in a just the few swims that had been baited. This left most other swims barren of fish, and if you didn't have the money to compete in buying vast amounts of maggots, then the less fortunate anglers often blanked and complained. I fell into this category as I couldn't afford to buy that amount of bait, and I really didn't want to go down that path. I couldn't even afford a £1.50 day ticket for the upper stretch at the time and had to fish the cheaper lower section from the car park downstream that had a lower barbel population. The maximum amount of maggots I ever bought was 4 pints, to try it out. It didn't really work for me, although at times it did draw the barbel into the swims. It was great watching the barbel eat the maggots, which got my heart thumping and legs wobbling, but it wasn't great watching them eat every maggot in the swim, except mine. Although I did catch the odd one at times, it became very frustrating.

Eventually, to cut a long story short and to get on to the rolling and roving game, the best way I found to use maggots was in a feeder but different from the norm, and it happened by accident!

It wasn't until I decided to fish the Trammels that feeder fishing for me came into its own, and boy, did it work! From that day on, I became proficient and very confident in my approach and everything clicked. At the time, I used two other methods, trotting and static ledgering, with a set-up rod for each. I was still at the stage where my catches were limited to only one or two fish a day. When I was on holiday, I was lucky and very happy to get ten barbel in a week. In the later years through the 1980s, when I became very confident, I would expect to catch on average between a minimum of 50–70 barbel in the same period of time.

My transformation began on a day when a local lad had walked around the fishery and came back and reported that a guy had caught three barbel from the Trammels. At this time I had never ventured up the fishery to this area because I could not afford the ticket. I was always led to believe that the area was very shallow with no flow, and therefore did not hold any barbel.

The Boathouse Swim on the upper stretch of the Royalty Fishery on the Hampshire Avon. This was one of the most productive swims in terms of 'bigger specimens' on the Royalty in the 1970s and 1980s.

It was about midday, very hot and sunny, and I had already bought a ticket for the lower section. What the hell! I decided to risk it and walk upstream to the expensive top stretch. I was looking at the Pipes and Watersmeet when I met the guy returning from the Trammels. I asked him, as we do, if he'd caught anything, and he told me that he had caught three barbel moving below the weir. Wow! This really got me going, as catching three barbel in half a day was exceptional at this time for me. As an added bonus, he was just leaving the fishery to go home! I didn't ask from what swim he had caught them but I swiftly and enthusiastically toddled up to the top end of the fishery to the weir, out of the way! I was constantly looking over my

shoulder for the bailiff, as well as looking to see if I could find the swim, but the untrampled bank-side vegetation was not going to give it away.

At first, I started trotting with maggots about mid-stream along 'Edwards', which is situated at the run-off from the Great Weir. I did get bites but I couldn't hit them as they were too quick and a long way downstream. So I moved a few yards further down to where I got the bites, thinking that I must have a better chance of connecting. Since they were so quick, I thought they must be dace and I still couldn't hit them, so I moved again until I was directly in front of where the float was going under. With no luck, I thought I might stand a better chance by using a feeder that would stop still. The swim I was fishing, although I didn't know this at the time, was called 'Hayters', albeit at the end of it, at the downstream point of the island. I quickly changed to the other rod and filled up my little green feeder with maggots. I cast slightly upstream about two-thirds of the way across, near to where I had the bites on float. Unexpectedly, the current swept the feeder downstream as it was not heavy enough to hold bottom. I was still holding the rod at the time, ready to put it onto the rod rest, when I could feel small taps coming through the rod and line. Again, thinking that these were small dace having a go at the maggots, I didn't take much notice and just placed the rod in the rest. The reason I did this was that everyone, including me, was led to believe that if a barbel took the bait, it would literally pull the rod in. This was often the case at the time and it was not uncommon for rods to go flying along the bank or even get pulled straight into the river; I saw it happen time and again. Anyway, with my rod in the rest, the feeder carried on

moving a bit further and something in my mind told me to try striking at the small taps. I picked up the rod and struck, and woe betide, I latched onto something a lot bigger than a dace. At first, I thought it was a chub but then it showed some serious power as it darted to the far bank rushes. I was using a Normark 12ft float rod at the time, and as soon as it bent over, I knew what it was. My legs turned to jelly as it was a bit of a shock and it felt big, but I played the fish out and landed a nice barbel of 5lb 6oz. I was over the moon as I had caught the barbel on the first cast with the feeder! I thought, 'Have I stumbled on the swim the bloke had three out of?'

After returning the fish, it clicked in my head that I had caught that barbel while the feeder was moving, and I hadn't put enough weight on to anchor it in the swim! I filled up the feeder with maggots and tried it again! With a repeat of the same small knocks, I decided to strike and I was into another barbel. I caught three barbel in three casts. This was amazing as it had never happened to me before. The swim

The Trees and Rushes Swim, now called the 'Stumps' is a tremendous area of the Royalty where you can roll, trot or fish while remaining static. The area is above the Pipes and at the bottom of the Parlour.

Ray Walton in action on the Aldermaston Mill Fishers on the river Kennet in Berkshire. This is a superb place for roving and rolling, especially on the 'Lawns' swims and in the 'Weirs'.

had a lot of weed on the far bank as well as in the middle with open, narrow channels and a drop off at the head.

Later in the afternoon, the flow slowed down and although I didn't know why at the time, the cause was found to be that the water company weir keeper had closed down one of the main gates in the weir pool. This caused the weed to come to the surface and also a change in the direction of the current. For some reason, the bites and fish stopped coming. I could now see into the water quite clearly as it was fairly shallow. I began to pick out some black shapes slowly cruising up and down on the gravel, in and out of the weed on the far bank. These were definitely chub, with the odd longer barbel. There was just enough flow to cast the feeder upstream and let it move down into the swim through the channel. I started to throw maggots as far as I could, across to the far bank, to see if I could get the barbel interested again, but the chub went mad for them and started taking them off the surface. I did notice that there were a number of casters in my maggot box and thought that maybe the chub were going for them and not necessarily the maggot in particular. It stayed quiet for a long time and I stopped catching, which seemed to coincide with the closing of the weir gates.

About an hour went by and the weed started to move from side to side again and the flow started to increase. They had opened the gate again and would you believe it, I caught another barbel. It was amazing, and I carried on catching, quite frequently until I ended up with twelve in all, plus one chub. I individually weighed each fish and wrote down the weights on a piece of paper when I realized that after about the fifth barbel, this was probably going to carry on to be something special.

The fact is, I caught the majority on the 'moving' maggot feeder. Over the next two days, I totted up another thirty-four barbel, the biggest being 9lb 9oz. In all, I ended up with forty-six barbel and one chub, weighing in every fish and keeping a record of them. The total barbel weight was 238lb 10oz. I am also sure I had recaptures at the time as I began to notice marks on their bodies. I learnt a good deal about barbel bites, and also that the water and air temperatures played a part in catching. In fact, I learnt more about barbel in those three days than I had in the whole of my previous fishing life.

Soon after my feeder success, I stopped buying maggots and casters and concentrated on using cheaper luncheon meat, fished on a 'rolling' bullet, swan shot, and from 1991–92, 'plasticine', which I continue to use today as weight, with great success.

LET THE GOOD TIMES ROLL

Rolling and roving is a specific type of fishing that requires a good deal of practice to become consistent in catching. The more time you spend trying to perfect the method, the more successful you will become. You will have to be mobile in your approach and be prepared to hold the rod in your hand at all times when rolling baits. It is wise to travel light, as you will be walking and searching for barbel along the whole length of river you are fishing. By doing this, you will begin to feel more comfortable and learn about every area of the fishery and not just a few swims or hot spots. This will lead on to helping you become very knowledgeable and more confident in catching. When proficient with the technique, not only will you find out where barbel are holding up in unusual places on harder stretches, but you will begin to understand barbel movements over long distances and find them when they go missing at different times of the season. This should give you an edge

This 10lb 3oz barbel was caught at the Aldermaston Mill fishery on the 'Lawns' using rolling luncheon meat. Note the 'two-tone' feature of the fish.

over fellow anglers when river conditions change from season to season. It is useful to keep records of your catches by logging and photographing, so that you can identify individual barbel each time you may 'capture' and 'recapture' them in different swims along the stretches. It will give you a truer understanding of how many barbel are present, and also a more accurate reading of the amount of bigger specimens or doubles. This will stand you in good stead for the future as you will be able to analyse your captures and also watch the barbel grow and fluctuate in weight throughout their lives. From experience, I would recommend logging and therefore investing in a good quality portable dictation tape recorder or at least a notepad, a decent SLR, compact or digital camera, flexible tape measure and reliable weighing scales as 'part' of the necessary kit to do this. Even if you blank, it is still worth noting and mapping the areas where you fished and also times, weather conditions, and whatever you think may be of interest. This strategy is all part of the learning process to become successful.

ROVING KIND

To make your roving days less tiring and more enjoyable, you will need to travel light. That doesn't mean you should skimp on tackle, but rather choose reliable lightweight essential items and clothing in which to do your fishing. In my early days, I used to carry all of my tackle with me on to the bank, even though I hardly used most of it. You will soon get tired and fed up with walking around with the heavy loads strapped to your back or on your shoulder. It might eventually dampen your will to rove, and you'll plonk yourself down somewhere, cast out and fall asleep. Nowadays, most of my essential items are carried in a waistcoat, a tackle belt and a bum bag. If I have to walk a long way to a specific fishing area away from the car, then I will take a small light rucksack

Taking notes about your captures can be a great advantage and will enable you to become very knowledgeable.

This is part of Ray's tackle and accessories. He tries to restrict himself to carrying small, reliable items.

strapped to my back, to carry some food, drink and camera bits.

My main equipment and accessories for a session include, one rod, one reel and a spare spool loaded with line, Whitlock extendable-collapsible landing net, hooks, weighted hooks, small sharpening stone, knot picker, plasticine, heavy metal, non-toxic shot, forceps large and small, green marker pen, braid blades, combination tool, long disgorger, fabric tape measure, small magnifying glass, Hardy water thermometer, Savlon, Klin-ik antiseptic, plasters, rod rest, unhooking mat, Avon scales, large weigh sling, headlight and torch, batteries, camera/accessories and mobile phone. Clothing and footwear depend on the seasonal conditions, but include thermal long johns, jeans, Realtree fleece over trousers, thermal long-sleeved vest, woolly jumper, waterproof Realtree plastic suit, Columbia silent hunter coat, camo head fleece, woolly hat, camo cap, neck warmer, Barbour and Realtree fingerless gloves, thermal socks, Mukluk thermal waders,

Derri thermal boots, chest waders, stocking waders, Thinsulate thermal boots, all for colder or more wintry conditions. I wear a combination of these items according to the weather conditions. For summer, Realtree T-shirt, string vest, lightweight trousers, jeans, shorts, lightweight Realtree flimsy showerproof coat, long socks, stocking waders, stocking chest waders, sandals, beach boots and other bits.

ROLLIN' ON A RIVER

The first choice of venue is of paramount importance when you are 'new' to the roving and rolling method. You should be looking for stretches of river where there is a higher population of smaller and medium-size barbel and not necessarily specimens. Once you have mastered the method on these generally easier venues, then you can consider moving on to lesser populated waters with very big fish, if, of course, that is your destiny.

95

Down south, I think the river Kennet at Aldermaston, Padworth, Upper and Lower Benyons, and the Wasing Estate in Berkshire, St Patricks Stream and the river Loddon, the Royalty Fishery on the lower end on the Hampshire Avon in Dorset and Fishers Green on the river Lee in Essex, are excellent starting points. Various stretches on the Bristol Avon, such as Kellaways and Limpley Stoke, are also a good bet. Further up country, the rivers Teme, Severn and Wye also have some good venues to practise the method. On these higher barbel-populated stretches, there will be more of an element of competition for food and therefore the bite ratio will be greater than in the lesser populated areas. On venues with a lower population,

the bite ratio will be lower and may slow your progress. The higher bite ratio is essential at first as it will give you vital experience in bite detection and types of bites that are encountered. This will speed up the learning process. Some river stretches will be a better option than others in that they will have more open fields and little bank-side vegetation. On these types of venues, you can be more mobile in your approach and can sometimes rove and roll a single bait for over 100 yards of river or more in 'one cast' when searching out fish. Other stretches may be tree lined with gaps, have steep banks and other features that limit access to swims and may restrict your casting and rolling somewhat. Also, a sense of 'etiquette' must be applied

The river Wye is a good venue for rolling and roving. Ray caught two barbel on this river on his first attempt.

As can be seen in this picture, taken in the summer of 2002, Bob Church has climbed into the Great Ouse in pursuit of his fish. Whilst playing a big barbel Bob thought it better to get into the river in order to keep the fish away from the snags.

Bob Church with a superb 13lb 8oz barbel taken from 'Top Hole' on the Great Ouse. The fish looked 'almost like porcelain'.

The Great Ouse at Adams Mill in flood conditions.

Pete Reading with a superb 15lb 5oz barbel he caught on the Great Ouse on maggots.

This photograph shows what Guy Robb's 'snowman rig' looks like in water. The rig uses two half-boilies, one made from a pop-up mix and the other a standard mix.

Guy Robb's hair-rig for cagey barbel. Note the heavy lead, the small hook, tiny bait and how difficult it is to see the hook link.

The same rig as illustrated above right with a shadow showing up the hook link.

This photograph illustrates why Guy Robb prefers to use clear line as opposed to braid or coloured lines.

As this picture shows, stone ledger weights offer extremely good camouflage although the swivel is still clearly visible.

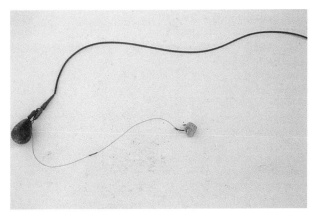

Guy Robb disguises his line with green rig tubing so that the line looks like a strand of weed.

These pictures illustrate Guy Robb's reed rig that can be used effectively near reedbeds. A reed is slit with a knife so that the line can be hidden within it. Note the use of green, garden bag ties and how well camouflaged the rig is in the picture, bottom right.

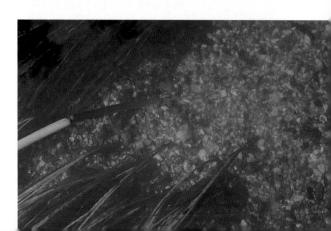

A shoal of barbel that Guy Robb spotted in the Bristol Avon.

Large barbel eagerly eating John Baker's mix on the River Avon.

The Parlour Pool on the Royalty Fishery on the Hampshire Avon. This was the scene of many catches of 'barbel in quantity'. The Garden Swim and the overhanging willow were two of Ray Walton's favourite swims for stalking and rolling.

Ray Walton with a personal best barbel weighing 18lb 13oz 8dr that was caught on the Great Ouse on spam. The rolling method works everywhere and results in the capture of big fish as well as smaller ones.

Steve Curtin with his wonderful 19lb 6oz 8dr barbel named Red Belly. Steve caught this then-British record barbel on the Great Ouse on 27 October 2001 when the fish was in its heyday.

Trevor Wilson holds the barbel that was rejected as a record-breaking fish.

Paul Bennett's superb 14lb 4oz Ribble barbel that was just 3oz off the river record.

Tim Ellis with his majestic 17lb 1oz Wensum record barbel that he caught on 8 October 2003.

Ray holds a nice barbel from the river Wye that he caught while participating in a Barbel Society fish-in.

When Ray began teaching his method of barbel fishing, his first pupil was Don Bird from Surrey who is pictured here rolling on the river Kennet.

Don Bird with a 5lb plus barbel he caught at the 'Lawns Swim' at Aldermaston Mill on the Kennet.

toward other anglers on the bank so as not to disturb or get too near to where they are fishing. If there are lots of anglers on the bank, you may be restricted and have to settle for a single swim at times, or try elsewhere.

READY TO ROLL

When you are kitted out and ready to rock and roll, the first main goal is to keep mobile and search the river trying to locate feeding barbel in the shortest period of time, unlike baiting up a swim and waiting for the barbel to come to you. Instead of the usual static fishing approach where you set up your tackle in one swim and bait up a specific spot, this time you will be waltzing along the riverbank, walking forward, backward and sideways, wide awake with anticipation expecting a fish to jump onto

your offering in every swim and area you may select. In other words, you'll never get bored as when having to sit in one spot and especially when the barbel are not playing ball. You will optimize your chances of catching by moving around.

The name of the game is to present a one-off 'single' bait into every good and unlikely area of the river, looking for 'opportunist' barbel; also, trying everywhere will develop your watercraft skills that after a while, help you find the barbel instinctively.

On most occasions, I am searching for barbel that have not been made too cautious by pre-baiting, and are alert to the fact that loose freebies get washed off baited swims by the current and travel with the flow into a barbel safe haven where they feel confident. In my experience, if you locate this type of confident barbel in a relaxed state of mind, you will catch them instantly, usually on the first or second cast on the introduction of your bait. In practice, what I am trying to do is to present a rolling bait, usually luncheon meat or Spam, in the most natural way that a barbel would expect to see it in a flowing river. As an experiment, if you throw in a piece of luncheon meat, it will sink and roll along the bottom, gradually inching its way downstream, eventually getting caught up in natural obstructions such as the front of weedbeds, depressions, back eddies, debris or snags. The barbel have learned that these stopping points are convenient food stores or larders at times, and will include them in their patrol routes, or they will be lying in wait in close proximity, watching for a 'snack' to enter their domain.

In rivers with lush flora and fauna, the barbel's main cover or home is lying underweed beds, but it will vary from river to river, stretch to stretch and swim to swim. My favourite tactic would be to roll and present my bait along the weed channels,

John Stack on the Royalty fishing above the pipes at the Stumps.

under overhanging trees, or where I think they are resident. The offering moves into its path, onto its doorstep or into its home. The presentation must be executed with 'finesse' and with complete control to be assured that the barbel will be confident enough to intercept and grab it immediately. If you present it wrong and haphazardly, you will spook the fish and then have great difficulty in catching any. Notwithstanding this, even if you present correctly, you may find some barbel are a bit more wary, especially if they have been caught out before.

If I have not had a take or an indication that tells me that the barbel are present or interested, then I will move pretty quickly on to another swim or area. I might only

stay as little as five minutes covering my chosen spot before moving on. If I am trying a 'noted' swim, where I know barbel live or frequently visit, but they are not showing at that particular time, then I will return later in the day to try again. This is called 'rotating' the swims. It is possible that the barbel at this time are not at all interested, are not fully wound up and awake or may have been 'spooked'. If they don't intercept the bait after rolling through a number of times covering the near, middle and far bank, do not persist and 'flog' the swim, as this will only put the fish down further if they are present. Return later!

Sometimes the barbel have to be 'motivated', and by using your self-discipline in

This picture shows
weedy channels
and clear gravel,
the perfect
conditions for
rolling baits and
spotting barbel.

leaving the swim alone for a while, they may become active, alert and ready for action when you return. If you are unfortunate enough to have a bite, but miss it and get nothing, rest the swim and try again later. Quite often, I have left a swim for fifteen minutes, or less, and returned to catch immediately. However, I usually leave it longer.

ROLL WITH IT

It is important to cast upstream at a clock position of about 11 and let the current move the bait naturally downstream rolling along the bottom, while you are holding the rod at all times. This is achieved by leaving an element of slack in the line where a bow will appear. You must stay in touch with the end rig but not on a tight line, as this will spook the barbel if investigating and encountering resistance from the rod tip and tight line. Always keep the rig and bait on a relatively slack leash as it comes toward you, but take up the excess as necessary, giving and taking line as the current and direction dictate. I stress, do not fish a tight line. The reason is that the barbel may well have been caught before and will investigate the bait with a bit of caution, mouthing and tugging it an inch, to feel for resistance. If it does this, and senses that something is wrong, it will drop it instantly and move away. To overcome this, if you detect the pick-up and you sense that the barbel is 'testing' you, then give it an extra foot of slack, where hopefully it will gain confidence and grab the bait more firmly. This sometimes allows the bite to progress and for you to strike more confidently.

Good presentation is by keeping the rig upstream or parallel and roving the bank from swim to swim. If the rig goes past you, then catch up by walking downstream or give line before the flow tightens it up and lifts the bait off the bottom, which will pull the baited rig across to the near bank. By keeping the rig on the same course and track as it rolls downstream, you can search different areas of the river with subsequent casts, that is, the far bank, midstream or near bank, thus searching out where the barbel are hiding up. If your fishing bank is tree-lined, then you have to drop into the gaps between the trees and work the area in front of you, casting upstream, and following the same principle as mentioned.

Perfect presentation is keeping the rig moving slightly slower than the speed of the current that will vary at different spots and swims along the river. Changing the speed of the baited rig is essential to be consistently successful in fooling the barbel into picking up the bait. This can be gained by 'adding and taking away' shot, plasticine or other form of weight, to slow down or speed up the rig accordingly in each swim or area. When you get it right, your mind will be in the river with the fish, knowing every nook and cranny where they are hanging out and also what is happening to your bait.

ROLL IT OVER

Pull 8–10in of line away from the bottom eye of the rod and the reel, and hold it 'loosely' between the thumb and forefinger. Lay the line over the fingertip, running down alongside to the first finger joint. Bite detection is registered through the line, transmitting pick-ups and any bite indications back to this sensitive top part of the finger. With the rig weighted and presented correctly, every bounce, movement, pick-up and stop, are readily recognized. With a bit of practice and with more experience, your brain will learn to

Hold the line between your thumb and forefinger to detect bites.

decipher which of the tell-tale signs is being sent and whether you should strike or not.

My 'secondary' indicator is the rod tip, and I only use it when I am not 100 per cent sure why the rig and bait has stopped rolling. I then look for tiny giveaway signs that will tell me if it is a 'genuine' barbel enquiry. At first, it is worth striking at anything unusual, apart from the general feel one gets when familiarizing onself with the contours and obstructions on the riverbed. As practice, try rolling a rig and bait along a shallow barren stretch of river where you can see the gravel and weed, and watch the rig and bait's performance as it rolls along the bottom. This will give you an insight into what is going on, and will teach you a whole lot, especially on rivers that run gin-clear in summer.

In coloured water, either being natural or caused by rainfall runoff, although I cannot see what is happening underwater, I present the rolling bait in exactly the same way. Some of my best catches have

come at this time, especially in high-water and flood levels when I can't make out anything at all.

The barbel, once caught a few times by this method, will begin to wise up somewhat and you will have to carry on developing your bite detection skills. The 'touches' and 'pick-ups' will become virtually indistinguishable from latching onto bits of weed and stones. The barbel doesn't usually 'bolt' off at great speed on this method as they do with statically presented baits or when hooking themselves up on hair-rigs. When static fishing, it is intended to draw a barbel away from its home into your swim. If it picks up your bait, it will often bolt back to where it lives. That is why your rod will arch over or be pulled out of the rod rest, whereas in rolling, you are presenting the bait into the barbel's home, and as the barbel regards this as a safe place, it will only have to move a few inches to intercept the bait, sometimes eating and swallowing on the spot. They won't normally bolt, because it is already at

The barbel will be watching and testing your bait as it rolls through the swim.

home, if you get my drift. If spooked for any reason or your presentation is incorrect, it will just release and drop the bait on the spot and you will be none the wiser! At first, you may not recognize the more cautious pick-ups and put-downs as they are quite difficult to detect. You will find that a barbel picks up the piece of luncheon meat with the lips, so when you get even the tiniest enquiry, it is probable that the bait is in the mouth and being checked out. If it feels something is not right, it will eject it on the spot without moving off or bolting. When static or semi-static fishing, these bites are indicated by a small tap or pull on the rod tip, often associated with a dace bite, and mostly ignored by barbel anglers. That is how clever some barbel have become, and you can see this happening if you have the opportunity to 'sight' fish when the river is gin-clear, especially in summer.

YOU'RE SO STATIC

I may have given the impression that I never static fish, but that is not the case. I fish static and still hold the rod. While roving and rolling, I will encounter low-flow conditions, come across pools, slacks, eddies and slower spots close in or behind overhanging trees or obstructions in the river. These again are natural spots in which 'freebie' food items would be deposited on the bottom, or get caught up in the continuous circling of the current-forming eddies. Barbel will patrol these areas as they do others. Again, 'opportunist' barbel can be lying in wait on the edge of a slack or crease of the main flow, not necessarily in the slack, but watching and waiting close by. If the 'freebie' gets pushed or pulled into the eddy or slacker area and settles, the barbel will often follow

103

it in and pick it up in a matter of seconds, or maybe a little longer at times, as it susses out the situation.

In this type of swim, it is wise to slightly change your tactics. Approach with stealth and get yourself in a comfortable position and mode, and be patient. In slacks, it is wise to cast well upstream into the main flow and manoeuvre your rig and bait into the slack as carefully as possible, taking up line if necessary as it comes toward you. I have to say again that it is very important that you always leave the element of slack line so that the current continues to move the bait to the natural stopping points where the barbel would expect to find it. If you put the rod down or fish a tight line, you may blow your chance if it picks up and feels for resistance. Sometimes, a crafty barbel will test the offering two or three times, picking it up and putting it down on each occasion. I often feel that these types of bites are not showing enough to strike, but this can often be a mistake on my part! It can then become a battle of wits between you and the barbel, and who makes the first mistake. Don't forget, give it a bit of controlled slack line!

Wayne Stevens engaged in stalking and semi-static fishing on St Patrick's Stream in Berkshire.

If a number of barbel are present and they are not spooked, this can create an element of competition where they can lose all inhibitions and their normal sense of caution. I have seen barbel in a confident mood where you would think that they were communicating with each other and playing in a happy game of 'dare' where they would spur and tease each other on into picking up my static luncheon meat hook-bait, seemingly knowing that there was that element of risk involved. Again, this has to be seen to be believed! If one of the group begins to get edgy and shows it by backing off or bolting, or even picks up the bait lightly in the lips, then drops it, then others will sense the reaction and spook. If you leave your bait in the same position as though nothing has happened, they may return for a second go and the same procedure will take place, although they may be more cautious, until eventually one has the 'bottle' to go all the way and munch it. Pay particular attention at this time as you will have to strike when the barbel's head moves over the meat and mouths the bait. All you will feel, if anything, is a tiny pick-up or tap, but at this time the barbel would have lifted it into its lips to test it. Strike immediately if detecting any indication, or when the meat disappears from view. Don't wait for a normal bite to materialize and progress, otherwise you may be too late and the barbel will suss you out, and back off again out of the swim.

ROVING EYE

When roving in summer and sometimes in winter, you will often be able to spot the barbel in the river. This is a great opportunity to experiment and watch their behaviour patterns when you present new baits and rigs. Not least, fishing for them is brilliant. If the river is low with hardly any flow, I will often stalk the fish still using a single bait. Without the flow, it is difficult to roll with satisfaction, and therefore I may have to take off any weight on the line and then use totally free lined bait on the hook. If there is a slight flow, I will use a specially prepared 'heavy metal' weighted hook, if I feel it is necessary to get a better presentation.

If I spot barbel in these conditions, I will at first watch if the barbel are moving around and if so, plot any possible patrol routes. I will place a 'static' bait accordingly along that patrol route or somewhere in the vicinity.

If the barbel locate the bait and are confident that where I have placed it is safe, I can usually guarantee an instant pick up, just as with rolling. Hopefully, I am looking at the opportunist barbel that do not have any sense of caution. If they are cautious and have been fished for consistently, my task will be that much harder and I will work on them trying alternative baits, and sometimes adjusting the length of the rig.

One good tip though, if a barbel does approach the bait to within, say, a foot in distance and then backs off, *don't* move the bait immediately. If it approaches a second time and does the same again, then you know it is interested. From experience, then, a simple repositioning of the bait may do the trick. Sometimes, if you totally remove the meat from the water, the barbel returns and is bewildered to find it gone! It will then go looking for it, trying to find where it is. Placing it nearer to the weedbed, or even amongst the weed out of sight is a good bet, as is placing the bait downstream behind the fish, but don't do this when the barbel is present as it may be watching you. It could take some time and be a game of trial and error. When the barbel do not co-operate, it is time to move on and return later. Sticking it out can result in a serious deflation of confidence.

The reasons why you don't catch visible fish in your swim can be manyfold, including such common things as the fish being spooked by the line, rig, bait and anglers on the bank. Other less obvious reasons could be that they are asleep, have already fed and are satisfied, have been caught recently or from the same spot before, are feeling wary, are nocturnal feeders, have specific feeding times, feed on natural river macro invertebrates or small fish, are stressed out due to water quality and temperatures, weather pressures, angling pressure and so on. There could be a combination of factors but the bottom line is that they 'will' eventually have to feed to survive. When, however, is another question!

VANTAGE POINT

The most exciting mode of fishing that you will encounter when roving is when you stumble across visible barbel. Wherever and whenever you can spot the barbel, it will be of great advantage to you in stalking the fish, watching their patrol routes, feeding habits and reactions to your baits.

Higher banks are generally the best points to look down from into the clear water, especially through polarizing sunglasses to aid visibility. Low bridges are also a good choice if you can gain access to them. Overhanging trees are very popular but you have to be very careful with your footing. If you are contemplating fishing from these points, you must predetermine the safety aspect and risk assessment to

Spotting barbel is advantageous because the location of the fish is half the battle.

yourself as they may be quite dangerous. Also, it may be impractical or even prohibited.

The most ignored vantage point is probably close in under your feet, if there is deeper water present, where the barbel can swim tight to the bank. Groins that jut out from the bank to divert the flow are another good example. You may need to lie down on the bank to take full advantage of these points. Barbel in some rivers, feel much safer when swimming very close to the banks where there is little midstream weed cover or underwater features, and also where there is a greater depth, and cover provided by bank-side rushes, under-cuts, tree roots, metal and wooden piles, snags, overhanging trees and caught-up debris forming rafts. Placing baits closer in can be far more productive than fishing further out in these situations. The good thing about fishing close in is that the closer the barbel comes, the less they can see you, as their vision is restricted to a point where they can only see the side of the underwater bank. They appear to be more confident and less cautious, as they may not have been hooked there before. A lot of inexperienced or unsuspecting anglers will 'accidentally' catch barbel close in. More likely, they will have their rods pulled over when they leave their baited rigs at the water's edge when having a cup of tea or a jimmy riddle. If you think about it, the majority of anglers, including pleasure anglers, match anglers and specialists alike, throw leftover bait down in the edge of the river at the end of the day. Common sense tells you what happens next! Later on in the evening or at night as the barbel become more active and mobile, they will search for food and eventually find and mop up the freebies, and most importantly, they won't be hooked or spooked in any way. This will give them renewed confidence, especially if they have

been caught previously. I have found that the barbel feel very confident in picking up single baits close in. The further out you fish in the river toward the midstream, the more chance barbel have of spotting the angler on the bank, as their vision is refracted on the water's surface. Although they won't necessarily bolt or move out of the area, they will still behave more cautiously when they are aware of you being there. It doesn't mean you won't catch them, but it may prove a little more difficult and your presentation may have to be spot-on to entice the barbel to your bait. Despite what you may read in books or magazines about barbel not having the ability to remember things, in my opinion, some barbel definitely learn from their mistakes and wise up pretty quickly.

As mentioned before, on high banks where you can easily spot fish, it becomes very tempting to present a bait to try and catch one immediately. You will have to put on your thinking cap and consider the pitfalls of such areas. They might look good, with barbel swimming about in the weed and easily seen, but you also have to consider two important things. First, is it possible to land the fish when hooked? The bank might be too steep and your landing net might be too short. There may be trees below or obstacles that the fish could run into and snag up, and you have no means to retrieve them, and you could possibly leave them tethered. Second, even if you do land a fish, can you get down the bank to return the fish safely? Is there somewhere close by to do this? These things must be pre-planned and the ultimate safe return of the barbel to the water is paramount. The only conclusion is, if there is no place to land or return the fish, then don't even attempt to fish for them in the first place!

When high bank roving and rolling, the most important thing is to know *where* in

A choice of different brands of luncheon meat is advised for summer and winter fishing.

advance, you are going to land the barbel, even if the only access point is down the bank a hundred yards away, where the barbel can be played and guided safely to the landing point downstream. Guiding the fish upstream to a landing point is a bit more difficult but not impossible, if the heavier line strength I advise is used.

One thing I have learned over the years is to try and do everything yourself whenever you can, and don't rely too much on others, even though it can make things easier on occasions. Become as capable as possible and experience the confidence and self-satisfaction in being self-sufficient. If you go roving on your own, then you would have to learn and be prepared to do it all, with nobody's help!

LOVELY SPAM

Luncheon meat has been used as bait for at least forty-odd years and still catches barbel very consistently today. To use the Royalty as an example, I have used the pink stuff as my number one bait continuously for at least twenty years. On the Royalty in the 1980s and early 1990s, I used a minimum of three or four 14oz tins of Tulip and Celebrity and other brands in a typical daytime session. Originally, I used to buy the cheapest available from the Cash and Carry, simply because I needed so much. Olde Oak, Plumrose, Celebrity, Tulip, Co-Op, Princes, Spam, Bacon Grill, and others, have all caught well for me over the years. Luncheon meat and chopped ham and pork have accounted for 99.9 per cent of my captures over the past twenty years, including my 1998–99 British record of 17lb 4oz and more recently others of 18lb 13oz 8dr, 17lb 12oz and 17lb 3oz. All of these big fish captures have come on a single chunk of unflavoured 'Spam' in winter. All other captures from 3lb–15lb 14oz from all rivers fished over the past twenty years have been on single chunks of luncheon meat, Spam, meatballs or Sensas-flavoured meats. Sensas-flavoured coloured type meats are brilliant and have their day! Campbell's meatballs work well but are messy and you usually need a large boilie needle to threadle them on the hook. Garlic sausage also works well but I can't stand the vile smell and therefore never use it. Liver sausage, chicken, chicken skin, Pepperami, chipolatas, sausages, raw sausage meat, corned beef, dog and cat food are just some other meat baits that work and are worth trying.

The leakage factor, as in modern paste and boilie baits, is said to be an important attractor to barbel, but with meat I don't think barbel are that particular, as most tend to know what it is and eat it on 'sight' when presented well, whether fished static or rolling. In the summer, if the temperature was very hot, I sometimes used five or six tins depending on the heat, which dictated how often it came off the hook when casting, as well as how many fish I caught, or unwittingly missed on striking. All this resulted in losing the bait, even when hooking a fish, as the meat is nearly always ejected by the fish on striking. Even though I never intend to pre-bait or bait a swim with luncheon meat, when it accidentally comes off the hook, I am unwittingly pre-baiting, albeit in a freebie sense where the meat will float off downstream in midwater over the heads of the barbel.

Eventually, it will sink, roll and stop at the roots of a weedbed or snag somewhere, or even be taken by a barbel on the move! When it does float off downstream, the barbel don't usually rise and take it midwater except on the odd occasion. However, they do see it and they will be aware of the pink stuff coming down in the current at that particular time and will ultimately put themselves into an alert response mode and be ready to intercept the next piece, if presented nearer to, or hard on the bottom!

If a barbel does intercept and eat a loose freebie that has come off your hook, then there is a very good chance that it will be 'satisfied' and will become one less fish that you will catch at that particular time of day. In winter, it could satisfy the individual for the whole day or even longer! However, I have witnessed barbel take a second piece of about one inch square in a short period of ten minutes in summer but, generally, they are quite clever and don't risk a second attempt for a while. When a barbel is in a happy mood in summer and oblivious to any danger, it will feed freely and do things out of the ordinary. They used to do this in the Royalty's Parlour Pool under the chain, where they would take food items from passers-by and anglers off the surface without any inhibitions. In fact, I once accidentally dropped a whole strip of meat in the water of about 4in long × 1in thick and a barbel came up in mid-water and ate it whole! On another occasion, a couple of mates and I witnessed a 'single' barbel eat a whole tin of meat that we fed over a period of about an hour – all 1in cubes taken in mid-water.

Below the Parlour's turbine house there was a restricted area set aside by a chain which spanned the width of the pool. Originally, it was a sanctuary for the salmon as they migrated upstream. They used to use the salmon ladder on the right or the gap in the wall left, when the water levels rose with an influx of rainwater. If the levels were low, the salmon would wait in the pool in the vicinity of the sanctuary, where a strict fishing ban would be in force, to protect the vunerable kings of the river. The water passed through the turbines and emerged from under the turbine house that created turbulent water with eddies that, for some reason, the barbel loved and they could often be seen in small groups swimming in and out from under the turbine house or kiting hard up against the stanchions and even coming up onto the shelves when the water levels rose. The amazing thing about these barbel is that they would feed, usually without hesitation, on the bottom, mid-water and unbelievably off the surface, competing with other barbel, ducks, swans, chub and small fry and huge 20lb–30lb carp. In summer, some of these barbel would eat cube after cube, every day, sometimes returning at 15-minute intervals for seconds or more. It is another of those exceptional things that you would have to see first-hand to believe. Barbel seem to be more adaptable to different river environments and conditions where they do things out of the ordinary in some places but not in others!

The pink square cube of luncheon meat has always been the standard shape to use, even going back all those years. Today, it is still the same and it still catches on all rivers. In national surveys, luncheon meat still produces more barbel over the season than all other baits. Boilies, pastes, pellets, cheese, maggots and so on still catch, of course, but luncheon meat is still the most reliable in my opinion. I've seen anglers shape it into triangles and use it with a punch, and they all believe it catches more than the square. Even very small squares or bits are very effective. Although I still use big pieces, I remember a time in the

Royalty's Railway pool a while back while rolling when I used up all the chunks and strips of meat in my pocket. I only had scraps left. So I had to drop the hook size and use the bits, and I must admit that I was not at all confident at the time that they would work. I was absolutely amazed at continuing to get the bites and still catch barbel just the same as with chunks. As the session went on, I used smaller and smaller pieces to make it last, until I ran out and left for home.

The pink stuff is seen by barbel in our rivers year after year, flowing down in the current or anchored to the riverbed throughout fisheries. All generations of barbel that are alive today, big and small would have encountered it at some time, and even possibly passed on knowledge about it through hereditary factors. With its consistent use over time, it is my opinion that luncheon meat has become like a natural, and is seen as an everyday dietary food supply. Barbel, as well as other species eat it, albeit with known hazards and risk factors attached. I have caught pike, chub, bream, eels, salmon, sea trout, rainbow trout, dace, tench and carp, all on luncheon meat and all from barbel-inhabited rivers.

On highly populated fisheries where there is competition for 'fast food', some barbel have cleverly learned to hit the pink on sight, without smelling, tasting or checking it out first. The thought is, 'If you don't grab it first, then someone else will'. I've caught them on a slow sinking 'pink' marshmallow in mid-water, and rolling a 'pink' piece of bath sponge! However, these were experiments and I think the real thing is still the best. You will be aware that there are loads of different brands of luncheon meat for human consumption that differ slightly in colour and consistency, and there are also several brands of flavoured and coloured luncheon meats

Break and cut the luncheon meat into strips and use a basic rig with a large chunk of meat on the hook.

specifically made for fishing. All will result in catches at sometime, but there are some things I have learned over the years by experimenting and using the different types. It has become highly important for me to choose the right brands for summer and winter fishing, but more to the point, hot and cold water fishing.

If you look at the ingredients on the tin, you will see that some will vary in meat and fat content. This will have a bearing on the consistency or texture of the product, making it a combination of hard, soft, bitty, fatty, greasy, spongy or crumbly. As mentioned before, when using the rolling technique, it is imperative to try to keep the bait on the hook and not lose a piece of meat on casting, striking or retrieving. The bottom line is that it will cost you fish at times if you lose it! There may only be a low number of feeding barbel in the stretch at the time, and losing the bait could be a determining factor in whether you catch or

blank. Also, as the barbel knows that there is a risk factor involved in grabbing the meat and has had a lucky escape, then the satisfaction is even greater.

When fishing on a hot sunny day in summer, you will find that your luncheon meat, will become very soft and greasy, and very difficult to keep on the hook. It's been a tradition to place a blade of grass or a piece of uncooked spaghetti on the bend of the hook to stop it pulling through and coming off when casting. Although this sounds practical and common sense, anything of this nature with the hook buried in the meat, can end up as a fish loser. It would, at times, prevent the hook pulling through the meat and penetrating the barbel's mouth when striking. In hot summer conditions, the easiest way to prevent any problems is to prepare your luncheon meat at home or beforehand, cutting it into strips or chunks, placing them in sandwich bags and then into a cool bag laced with ice

111

Ray Walton with a 9lb barbel from the Parlour Pool on the Royalty caught near the 'chain' on luncheon meat.

packs. If you forget your ice packs then it's best to leave your strips of meat in the sun; this will cook them and form a hardened crispy layer on one or two sides that will make them firmer and give the hook a better hold. Frying the meat at home in a pan is another tried and tested method. When roving, I have found that the meat can also get too warm if you are keeping it close to your body such as in your coat pockets or on a multi-purpose belt or neck apron bag. I personally don't have a problem in keeping the meat on the hook in summer, except on very long casts. Bigger-sized hooks, like sizes 2–6, will help enormously, but the name of the game is to keep the meat cool and to find the right brand and texture.

You will find by experimenting with different types of meat that they also vary slightly in colour, from a nice bright bathroom pink, fading to beige, depending on the brand. You may also notice that luncheon meat colour will eventually wash out and the meat become paler over a period of time in the water.

The purpose-made flavoured and coloured meats manufactured by bait companies also vary in texture and some brands are more preferable for barbel fishing than others. The colours and flavours are again both important. On some venues, some anglers will tell you that the barbel are spooked on pink luncheon meat and will run a mile on seeing it, or that they can keep barbel trapped in a circle of meat because they are too scared to cross the line to get out! To a degree, this can happen, and I have seen barbel bolt or totally avoid going near pink luncheon meat. It happens on most rivers at times, especially in open water and obviously when a barbel has had a bad experience. I know that most of the 'spooky' problems associated with the pink are down to presentation or baiting up. In my experience the 'same' spooky barbel will sometimes take the same piece of meat if it is presented in a different position, at night, in another swim or virtually anywhere on the fishery when not feeling very wary, as mentioned before. In fact, to prove the point, I have encountered the same sort of experience on the Royalty and elsewhere, and even with the very big British record barbel on the Great Ouse, notably 'The Pope' and 'Redbelly'. Although I have watched both fish shy away from my offering of static pink luncheon meat on one day, I have still caught both fish more than once on other occasions on the same bait!

My strict rule on this subject is that when you present the meat to a visible single barbel or shoal, you have to seriously monitor the reaction of the fish. Some will take the meat as soon as it enters the water; this is very common whether I am fishing rolling or static. Others will totally ignore the pink meat and back off or even vacate the swim. I will try a few alternative tactics for sure, if I feel it is worthwhile, but I don't usually hang around for barbel that are not interested at that particular time. I'll move on and try and find some barbel that are.

In the warm summer months when the water is crystal clear and there are no barbel visible, it doesn't necessarily mean that they are not present or feeding. Quiet often you can unwittingly pass an area that looks devoid of barbel but in reality, there might be a number of fish hiding under the weed, in a snag or undercut bank. When barbel are out on the gravels, flashing, moving in and out of the weedbeds and channels, you can be pretty sure that they are up for it.

HOT RODS

The first rod I ever used when I was a kid was a 6ft black and white fibreglass spinning rod and I used it to float fish and ledger to catch small perch, roach and bream on Hampstead Ponds in North London. Then, a 12ft orange hollow glass rod called the Grebe, that I used on the River Lee Navigation to catch bleak, chub, tench, perch and other small species. My first rod for barbel was a brown glass 13ft Bruce and Walker CTM, recommended to me for trotting for barbel and was very popular and the best-selling rod of the time. Others I used were a Normark carbon 12ft, followed by a Hardy 10ft brown glass.

The rods I have used for rolling over the past twenty years have included trout blanks, North Western 11ft medium feeders and Bruce & Walker 11ft Hexagraphs of 1lb t/c and 1.4lb t/c, amongst others. All did the job very well indeed especially the Hexagraphs and there is very little out there on the market to match them, as they are high quality and expensive.

I have since tried and succeeded in fine-tuning my own new rods for the roving and rolling game, to what I think are the requirements needed to perfect and advance the method and take it to another level. My exclusive, English-made 11ft fishing tools have been designed in straight carbon by myself and Harrisons Advanced Rods. The blanks are amazingly thin, powerful and lightweight with approximate test curves of 1lb 3oz and 1lb 6oz, which to me are an important factor when rolling, stalking, sight fishing and static fishing. The sensitive tip/top section enhances the tiniest of bites from wise and crafty barbel, transmitting every enquiry, pick up and bite back to me, registering at the tip and also my index finger, travelling right down through the butt section to the receiving hand. The 'thin' lightweight design allows me to hold the rod in hand without effort and with less resistance from the wind throughout my fishing sessions, yet maintain the power to tame the hardest fighting barbel. Even in extreme river conditions throughout the changing seasons I do not feel it necessary to step up to a higher test curve, although a longer 12ft model would possibly be beneficial on some wider rivers to pick up excess slack line when rolling at distance. I have had great enjoyment catching all sizes of barbel, chub and other species on the rods, and have still found reserve torque in the butt to take on the largest of specimens when encountered. I designed the rod to be used with smaller and lightweight fixed spool reels as well as the 'side casting' Rolling Pins/Mk1 and Mk2. The rods have a perfect balancing point around 2–3in above the 22in cork handle, subject to reel placement on the moveable reel fittings. I have eleven Fugi SIC single-legged stand off guides perfectly situated along the rod to complement and enhance the 'all through' action that travels right through to the butt. Not only does the rod bend in a perfect curve when playing a barbel, but also the single-legged stand-off rings bend fractionally and accordingly, thus creating a more forgiving and absorbing action that virtually eliminates bumping off big fish as they power off or when lunging at the net.

The combination of the slightly larger Fugi SIC rings complement the blanks through action, making the rods very versatile. With this combination of factors, it is possible to use a medium or heavier graded mono of 8–12lb b/s or equivalent diameter braided mainline of 20lb–30lb b/s. With the larger rings, I also get excellent casting distance and accuracy, free lined or with weighted terminal rigs. The rods have an unvarnished natural carbon smooth ground finish so as not to add extra weight and this helps prevent line stick when wet.

Although you can use various test curve rods and designs for the roving method, it becomes a personal choice and preference, and importantly, what you can afford. If you consider some of the design details mentioned, you won't go far wrong in your rod choice. One other thing is that you don't need to be 'overgunned' with a heavier and higher test curve when roving and rolling.

REAL TO REEL

Try and obtain a reel that is reliable, lightweight and balances the weight of the rod that you are using. This is necessary as your rod and reel combination will be top or bottom heavy and therefore you will have difficulty in holding the set up and presenting the bait satisfactorily. Your arm and shoulder may begin to ache after a while if the balance is incorrect.

In the past, I have used fixed spool reels including the small Mitchell 408 and progressed to the reliable Shimano GT 1000 with the rear-controlled fighting drag system. Newer and more expensive versions of this superb reel are still marketed and worth taking a look at. I also owned a 4in narrow drum Match Ariel, bought new back in the late 1960s for £6. I bought it to trot for barbel but ended up using it for occasional static fishing as I found it very difficult to use. Everyone who owned and used a centrepin told me how good they were for playing fish. When I started rolling baits as my favourite method, I remembered seeing very old pictures of side-casting centrepins and thought what a great idea they would be for my method of fishing. With that thought always in mind, an opportunity arose where I could design the reel of my dreams for roving and rolling baits. I took some advice from my mate, Colin Woods, who was a knowledgeable centrepin expert living in Dorset. He helped me draw up the design of the reel that was later to become 'The Ray Walton Rolling Pin' made by J.W. Young and Sons of Redditch and marketed by Bruce and Walker.

Today, I have not looked back or changed back to a fixed-spool reel. The 'Rolling Pin' is specifically built for the job and is a 3¾in, high-quality side-casting centrepin with a 1in wide drum that revolves 360 degrees at 90-degree intervals and allows accurate casting from the 'front', similar to a fixed-spool reel. With this concept, I have the ability to cast very long distances with ease, unlike a standard centrepin that I had problems with. After casting or hooking a barbel, I can switch it back to the normal position and play the fish as on a standard pin, which I find is more enjoyable and allows superior control. Many anglers talk about line twist on side-caster pins, causing tangles and affecting casting ability. At first when field testing the Rolling Pin, I did experience my new 8lb mono line looping on the spool, thus inhibiting my casting ability. Once the line had been used and lost its 'spring' effect and bedded in, the problem diminished and became less of a hindrance in continuous casting. Although you may get an element of line twist with mono, especially with 'new' line, it is only a minor problem, and can be alleviated by firmer controlling and laying the line across the spool when retrieving. When using a braided mainline of a similar diameter as 8lb mono such as Spiderwire, I don't get any line twist, or very little, as the line has no memory, is very limp and has virtually no stretch factor. I don't have any problems with braid, except perhaps when forgetting to control the line back onto the spool, thus causing a loose loop to appear.

The 'river roller' rods are my own design and are specifically made for rolling and roving. The 'rolling pin' revolves to the front for easy casting and superb control when playing barbel.

LINE UP

When I first started fishing for barbel as a novice, I was using 3lb Bayer Perlon mainline with a 13ft CTM and did not know any different. This was used on a small run-of-the-mill Shakespeare fixed-spool reel. I did catch loads of small barbel up to 6lb on this set-up but also lost just as many on line breakages. I remember a bloke on the Royalty in the early days using 10lb line and catching a 10lb barbel from Fiddlers. I, together with others, considered 10lb b/s as 'rope' at the time and it didn't give the fish a chance! Over the years, I upped the breaking strains using 4–5lb and being more comfortable with 6lb for a period of time. I caught a lot of barbel on this but still lost a good number and terminal tackle on snags and weed. Then came a time when I used Platil Soft and Platil Strong, a mono line which had a very low diameter with no stretch. It was thinner than other brands and it was great at first when new, but I soon lost confidence in it when it started deteriorating and breaking after catching a number of fish. Then I started using Maxima 6lb b/s, for feeder fishing and then progressed to 8lb because

Spiderwire is a braided mainline; it is no-stretch and very strong and sensitive to the smallest bites.

of weedy conditions and getting snagged and losing bigger fish. I caught consistently on this brand of line, but I still did not have confidence in landing bigger barbel, as it also sometimes broke when snagged and I had lost fish. Finally, I bought some thicker 10lb Maxima that gave me a lot more confidence and stopped my legs wobbling like jelly when I hooked a barbel. I began to hook and land the odd double-figure barbel without any worry that the line would break.

Today, my current preference is a braided mainline called Spiderline-Spiderwire Braid. Since changing to braid seven years ago, I have never looked back to mono. I started using it at 10lb b/s and experimented with 15lb, 20lb 30lb and 40lb b/s that is equivalent to 8lb diameter in mono. The reason for 'upping' the b/s is that I found in experimenting that it breaks well below its stated strength – that is, 10lb may well break at 6lb, 15 at 9lb, and 20 at 16lb and so on. I now use and am very satisfied with 30lb b/s that has the same diameter as normal 6lb–8lb mono. Because braid is thinner than mono, you will need the higher diameter and thickness to allow the river to 'tow' the line in the current and move the bait satisfactorily. With the higher strength of braid it also adds a massive confidence factor in knowing that you will land 99 per cent of hooked barbel, as I do nowadays. Another reason for using braid is that it has very little 'stretch factor' or 'memory' and is therefore highly sensitive to detecting bites, and you can feel every movement as the bait rolls along the riverbed. Everything is transmitted back through the braid, straight through to your index finger and tip of the rod. If you're not a braid man, then I still recommend a mono line strength of 8–10lb for fixed-spool reels or higher, preferably 'Maxima' but there are other good brands on the market. The choice is yours, but don't be tempted to fish light as you will lose terminal tackle and leave baited rigs in the water. Also, you may well get busted up and leave hooks in the barbel's mouth.

THE WEIGHT

I used to take it as the norm and expect to lose feeders and weights in snags, especially when a barbel took you into a weedbed and tied you up. You pull for the break and most of the time you will not only lose the fish but also your terminal tackle that includes the feeder, weight and hook. If the line breaks above the rig or you're using a bolt rig, you could possibly tether the barbel on the snag leaving it to die a slow, lingering death! It is in the majority of cases that the weight or feeder on the line is the cause of the problem, catching on the snag and hindering the safe retrieval of the barbel to the landing net. Not only this, but it is highly irresponsible for anglers to continue losing terminal tackle by using inappropriate rigs and line strengths or fishing near, or in, snags where they have no chance of getting the barbel out. Another problem that anglers don't seem to acknowledge, or have never even thought about, is cracking off on casting and striking, or snagging up and leaving fully baited rigs on the bottom. The consequences of a barbel picking up the unattached baited rig can be disastrous and can lead to the death of the fish if swallowed. Having experienced losing lots of terminal tackle in my early fishing years, I have since tried to lessen the problem. The first obvious thing to come to mind is to increase the line strength, and second, to eliminate what causes the rig to snag – that is, the weight!

My search for an alternative to the normal lead weights came about in 1990–91, and was a conscious and personal decision after two worrying occurrences while fishing in Walsham Weir on the river Wey in Surrey. At the time I was investigating the capture of one of the biggest barbel of the time by Jason Bailey, where he, his brother Martin and his dad were resident weir and lock-keepers. The brothers fished in the weir pool and after Jason's record barbel claim of 15lb 11oz in August was rejected by the British Rod Caught Fish Committee, Fred Crouch and I were given the opportunity to fish the weir pool to see if either of us could catch the monster barbel a third time to authenticate the existence of the huge fish. The weir pool was quite large with a controlled flow and was very snaggy with some underwater rocks and boulders at the head and downstream of the white water. It became more apparent as time passed that Jason and Martin were not experienced barbel anglers, which they would openly admit without hesitation. Their heavily weighted terminal tackle set-up was crude, to say the least, compared to my lighter approach, and they lost lead weights and hooks time and time again on the snags in the pool. It came to a point when I hated fishing there, as I lost a lot of tackle as well, and it became something of a nightmare. The final straw came when I caught a barbel with a hook in it's throat and weights hanging out of it's mouth, and this happened on two separate occasions. I knew at the time that none of us had been smashed up by barbel or hooked and lost a fish, so I had came to the conclusion that the barbel were picking up the snapped-off baited rigs left in the water. At this time, I decided not to fish the weir again until I could find an alternative substitute to fish the snaggy weir pool. I tried to obtain some angler's tungsten putty and tube but it was hard to find and soon after became discontinued. Snag Safe, or Heavy Metal was not around at the time, and even if they were they would have been too expensive to use in the quantity and weight needed. However, the latter would have been perfect if it had been cheaper, as it is similar to tungsten putty. While in the local sweet shop I spotted some very colourful strips of kids plasticine that cost around 60p. I bought some and went home to see if this was the answer to what I was looking for, although it was much lighter than lead shot. I didn't think the blue or yellow were the choice colours to use, so I started mixing the colours together to try and get a darker effect. It worked to a satisfactory degree and was acceptable as most of my weir pool fishing was at night. One problem with the sweetshop plasticine was that it got very hard as the air temperature dropped and was difficult to break off with cold fingers. It stuck to the line alright, but slipped down to the hook at times on casting and when catching on snags. But hey! This is the idea of using it! On my rig, it comes off when you get snagged up and pull for a break. You get your hook back nearly every time.

I found that if you hook a barbel and it runs into the weedbed or snag, it will generally be the weight or feeder that catches onto the obstruction. In this case it will be the plasticine, and if you do get snagged and pull for the break, the plasticine will slip down the line and be pushed off, and then you'll be in direct contact with the hooked fish so nothing else is on the line to snag you again. Although you'll find that you will still get caught up on the bottom when using plasticine, unlike shot that will pull down to the hook and lock up, thus eventually causing a break-off, the plasticine will come off freeing the rig or will slip down, pushing the bait off the hook, leaving it safe. There are three possible times when you will not retrieve the terminal tackle and one is when the point of the hook pulls into the snag itself thus rendering it safe! On occasions, it is possible

to straighten the hook on the snag when pulling for the break. If the breaking strain of the line is powerful enough, the hook may bend and you'll get it back for safe disposal. If the rig wraps itself around an underwater branch it is very difficult to retrieve unless the branch breaks.

On searching the shops, I did find a better alternative to the kids plasticine and this product is called Lewis 'Newplast'. It is non-toxic with virtually no smell or residue, reusable, softer, and comes in a multiple selection of colours obtainable in artist's supply shops. It is sold in approximately 12in × 2in × 2in stranded blocks, and costs around £1.60p. This is about 10–15 times cheaper than using non-toxic swan shot. Although it is not as dense as the other more expensive alternatives, if you add some fine sand to the product, it will make it heavier. It's great stuff and you can obtain a selection of colours and mix them to create a similar colour to the riverbed you are fishing. I mix two shades of brown to mimic the colour of gravel and pebbles and these can be moulded to any size or shape. More recently, although I begrudge buying heavy metal, I have succumbed to using it in small AA/BB-sized balls and mixing it in with the plasticine. This keeps the size of the weight smaller and thus helps it to stick to the line a bit better and also allows me to present the bait more effectively, getting more of a free-flowing roll down the swim with less snagging on the bottom.

SHOT AND SPLIT

Non-toxic split shot are the alternative to the now 'illegal' heavy lead split shot. They are not as dense as lead but are a harder metal, and some makes can break in half after a few uses. They can also pinch the line causing a weakness in the breaking

A selection of weights for different conditions and tactics.

strain, unless you protect the line with a sleeve. They are perfect for the rolling method in snag-free areas and using heavy lines or braid. They are more practical for rolling, especially in the bigger sizes like swan, double swan or even bigger, if you can find them in your tackle shop. Using the split shot aids the simplicity of the method in allowing the addition and sub-traction of the number of shot on the line, adjusting the weight for perfect presenta-tion. My personal view is that they work quite well in areas that are fairly clear of snags and dense weed. You will still catch fish on most occasions but you may lose a few as well, and also terminal tackle on occasions. Because of their bright silver-grey appearance, it is wise to wrap them in brown plasticine or colour them.

OFF THE HOOK

I use size 2 or 4, Drennan black-eyed boilie hooks that are reliable and perfect to use with a light through-action rod. They are somewhat thinner than the Drennan 'Continentals' and others and allow better penetration for the rolling method. I also bend the 'barb' back so there is just a 'nick' left. When experimenting in searching for the perfect hook for the method, I found that a great deal of brands of eyed hook have not had the 'eye' closed properly, and this can lead to losing fish due to the line pulling out, and/or cut your line! With a soft through-action rod, combined with the slack line element in rolling baits, it is wise to use a strong, slightly 'thinner' hook

119

as mentioned, especially at the point. Thicker hooks tend not to penetrate as well with a softer through-action rod and you may lose fish when bringing them to the net and when they make a final unexpected lunge. This is because you are unaware of playing the fish on the point of the thicker hook whence the barb has not penetrated the mouth efficiently and locked.

HOOK ME UP

I also modify some of my hooks of different sizes with soft, flexible weight as an added advantage for low-flow conditions. This allows a more delicate and effective form of presentation in that I can bury the added weight on the hook in the luncheon meat. I roll some Kryston non-toxic heavy metal around the shank of the hook and use shrink tube to cover and seal it. This allows me to eliminate any weight on the line. The normal weight, in slow flows, will hinder the natural movement of the bait. Therefore, the modification allows your bait to flow downstream more naturally in

'low flows' where weight on the line would keep latching onto the riverbed and snagging up. The weighted hook is a very effective item but you must strike on the first bite indication, as the barbel will not feel the resistance of the weight on the line if it intercepts and tests you. If you don't strike instantly, you stand the risk of deep hooking the fish. Also, I do not recommend that you use the weighted hook for static fishing and upstream static ledgering, for the same reason, unless you are confident and experienced. The barbel can pick up the bait and drop back, not feeling any resistance, and possibly run ten yards or more downstream without giving an indication of a pick-up because of the slack line. By the time the barbel takes up line downstream and your rod bends over, it would have probably swallowed the bait. Watching the line as it enters the water is a good way of early-warning bite detection in this situation. When using weighted hooks, hold the rod at all times. On some occasions, I will use a combination of both weighted hook and 'plasticine' on the line in certain conditions.

Drennan boilie hooks are Ray's preferred choice. Note that the weighted hooks are converted with heavy metal and shrink tube.

The Whitlock collapsible net fits conveniently on your shoulder. It makes life much easier and is practical for roving.

THE LANDING

After using various makes of fixed handle landing nets for over twenty-five years, I have now found the most practical tool for roving the banks. With the help of Graham Peplar of Davis Tackle in Christchurch we have redesigned a large collapsible 'Whitlock' salmon type with an added telescopic extension and a large barbel-friendly net that extends to 10ft. I carry the adapted model conveniently on my shoulder by means of a single, flexible bungee cord. This virtually eliminates any weight that you would undoubtedly carry and feel when grasping a fixed set-up net under your armpit and will therefore enable you to rove the banks comfortably and have a free hand at all times, while holding the rod in the other one. When you locate and hook a barbel, all you have to do is flip the bungee off your shoulder, grab the handle, and one end of the bungee will drop down, allowing the landing net to unfold, open and lock into position on its own accord. The conventional fixed handle alternative

The conventional landing net is awkward and impractical for roving.

is too heavy and inconvenient to lug around when roving along the bank. You would have to carry it 'set-up' and tucked under your armpit as I did at first. If it is windy, you will find it very awkward indeed as well as a pain in the neck when climbing over stiles and fences, especially if the net catches on barbed wire. I can tell you that my fishing has been so much more enjoyable and easier since using this model.

121

Brian Dowling

Brian Dowling is recognized as the country's acknowledged authority on the history, facts and figures surrounding barbel. It all began with the capture of his first barbel from the river Trent in the 1980s when he realized that he had found the species that he wanted to spend all his spare time studying.

After nearly twenty years of amassing all the available literature on barbel fishing, including hundreds of 'old' magazines dating back to the 1950s, he decided to store the information in A3 binders, indexing every article. In 1994 when the National Association of Specialist Anglers (NASA) required someone to compile a current Top 50 Barbel listing, there was only one candidate for the post. Brian added to and maintained the listing until 1999 when NASA merged with the Specialist Anglers Conservation Group. Around this time the Top 50 had become distorted with many recaptured fish from the Medway, Great Ouse and Wensum.

In order to provide a clearer national picture Brian originated a UK River Record Listing showing the largest barbel caught from over fifty of the country's rivers. This involved many hours of research, following up claims for big fish and investigating the never-ending flow of rumours associated with almost every river.

In this way, many previously unreported fish have come to light, and with the basic requirements of a photograph, have taken their place in the national records. The main sources of information have been those fish reported to the angling press and fish made available via the 'barbel grapevine'. The result has been the only authenticated record of large barbel caught in this country, with the angling press using this information as their form of reference.

However, when attempting to achieve such a 'definitive' document it must be stressed that there may be the 'odd' omission, due to individuals shunning the publicizing of their catches, or angling clubs imposing strict publicity bans. Brian hopes that readers will agree with him that despite this, it is far better to have a 99.9 per cent accurate 'historical statement' than none at all especially when detailed records for other coarse fish species appear to be almost non-existent. Hopefully, these records will provide barbel anglers everywhere with the inspiration to raise their own personal targets. When time permits, Brian enjoys fishing the smaller rivers for large barbel and to date has caught over sixty double-figure fish. In 1995, he was a founder member of the Barbel Society, a former member of the Barbel Catchers' Club and is at present records officer for the Ray Walton/Bob Church Barbel Specialists Group.

5 The Complete UK Barbel Record Lists

by Brian Dowling

BARBEL RECORD HOLDERS – PAST AND PRESENT AS AT 1 DECEMBER 2004

The requirements necessary for claiming a record barbel, or indeed any species of coarse fish, are nowadays clearly defined along established guidelines laid down by the British Record Fish Committee (BRFC) governing body in the UK.

Assistance is readily available from them for completion of the requisite claim form and for achieving the obligatory scales check carried out by Weights and Measures officials. Contact the BRFC on 01626 331330 for further details.

All of this is a far cry from the situation over 100 years ago when any record claim was often supported by the most flimsy evidence with weighing procedures often more to do with guesswork. Very few barbel records were actually kept then, and Wheeler's Thames barbel of 14lb 6oz caught at Moseley in 1888 was, for many years, assumed to be the largest of the species on record, despite the only evidence being three lines in the *Fishing Gazette*. That was until 1934 when the Hon. Aylmer Tyron fishing the Royalty Fishery on the Hampshire Avon, caught a barbel of 14lb 6oz equalling Wheeler's fish.

As this fish was mounted in a glass case at Tyron's home in Great Durnford, Wiltshire, it was considered to be the 'true record'. Since those days specimen barbel have been better documented, and within the following pages we take a journey through the history of record barbel and the fascinating stories, controversies and facts behind the figures.

CONTROVERSIAL LIST

The British Barbel Record list has often proved to be a controversial one, and the BRFC caused an outcry, when, in 1968 the existing record list underwent a major purge. Out went the previous barbel record, at the time held jointly by three fish at a weight of 14lb 6oz, these being

Happiness is a river Teme barbel. Brian with a 10lb 15½oz fish caught in March 1994.

Wheeler and Tyron's fish together with one caught by the well-known angler F.W.K. Wallis, again from the Hampshire Avon in 1937, the BRFC rejecting all evidence previously provided for the weighing and verification of these fish.

INTERIM MEASURE

Despite Joe Day's Royalty-caught fish (October 1962) being of lesser weight at 13lb 12oz, it was installed as the UK record, while the three fish at 14lb 6oz were being reinvestigated, with the BRFC intending to reinstate at least one of the three at a later date, thereby establishing a 'true' verified record.

However, these investigations proved inconclusive, leaving Day's fish at the top of the BRFC's record barbel list for the next twenty-two years, despite being considered as 'only an interim record'. Specimen hunters across the country respected both Tyron's and Wallis's fish, and accepted that 14lb 6oz was the weight to beat in order to achieve the record.

Because of this, record claims for both Martin Hooper's and Pete Reading's Stour fish at 14lb 2oz (incidentally the same fish) were never made official at their time of capture (1987–88) as both anglers recognized Tyron's fish as the one to beat. At the same time the National Association of Specialist Anglers (NASA) were maintaining their own listing of record barbel showing Tyron's fish as the UK's best.

Martin Hooper was encouraged by the angling press to submit a retrospective record claim to the BRFC in January 1990 as he had sufficient evidence in the form of two witnesses, specialist anglers Dave Tissington and Richard Graham and his scales had already been carefully checked for accuracy by Weights and Measures officials.

Pete Reading, on the other hand, chose not to forward a claim for his fish, as he had only one witness and his scales had not been the subject of the obligatory check.

BRFC–NASA LIST MERGER

Around this time (early 1990) a meeting held in London between BRFC and NASA officials resulted in the agreement to merge the freshwater record fish lists, thus ending many years of controversy.

Martin Hooper's fish caught from the Dorset Stour in October 1987, proved to be a temporary record, as, following the merger, the three fish previously rejected by the 'old' British Record Fish Committee in 1968 became the subject of further intense scrutiny. A previous investigation into these fish during 1971 had proved to be inconclusive.

However, with the merging of the two lists, Tyron's fish caught in September 1934 from the Hampshire Avon, was reinstated as the UK record in August 1990, mainly due to the painstaking research carried out by Fred Buller, the well-known fish historian. At this point the dust appeared to have settled with one freshwater record list recognized by anglers across the country and Tyron's fish reinstated.

Dave Williams of London provided a trio of barbel, two from the Hampshire Avon, both at 14lb 6oz and one from the River Medway in Kent, at 14lb 6½oz all falling for a secret paste bait, over an 8-day session in September 1992.

This appeared to have provided at least one fish to equal the 58-year-old record, but during November 1992, David Taylor, of Southwater, Sussex, fishing the Medway landed a fish weighing 14lb 9oz. This later proved to be the same fish as caught by Williams.

Two weeks later, David Taylor landed the same fish at 14lb 13oz. These fish were to become the subject of record claims, both eventually being awarded interim record status.

The New Year (1993) brought even more drama when Bob Morris, fishing the Medway at Fordcombe in January, caught and landed a barbel of 15lb 7oz, later to be pronounced as Britain's best. This fish named 'Bertie' by Fleet Street journalists, is actually a female and is the same fish that was caught by both Williams and Taylor.

In October 1993 the record was broken again by a fish of 15lb 11oz caught by Andy Harman, the location being described as a 'southern river', but press coverage revealed the location to be the Medway around Fordcombe – the fish responding to the name of 'Bertie'.

It was therefore no surprise when Pete Woodhouse from Leigh, fishing the Fordcombe stretch on the opening day of the 1994–95 season, caught 'Bertie' yet again, this time at a new record weight of 16lb 2oz.

All this has led to the widely held belief that many more of the largest barbel reported have been subject to recapture at one time or another, with their weight fluctuating considerably between captures. This complicates the overall picture regarding very large barbel, as it brings into question the true potential of many of our barbel rivers.

With both the Medway and the Wensum reporting very few big fish from the late 1990s onwards, it has been left to the Great Ouse to provide any potential record-breakers, with probably a dozen fish capable of reaching 19–21lb in weight within the next two to three seasons. Ten years ago, a 19lb barbel would have been laughed at, but even back in the 1940/50s fish estimated at 20lb were spotted in the Railway Pool on the Royalty Fishery by Mr M.W. Hayter the fishery manager.

Who would now wish to disagree with his sighting or that of Richard Walker and Fred J. Taylor in the 1950s on the Hampshire Avon, when a shoal consisting of five fish, the largest of which appeared to be at least 20lb, was kept in view for some length of time? Or the fish spotted by F.W.K. Wallis again on the Avon, and estimated to be around 20lbs in weight? With a Thames fish reported in the early part of the twentieth century at a weight of 23lbs who can doubt that fish well over the present record do exist?

The river Medway held the barbel record for over three years (1994–97) before the river Severn gave up one of its secrets in the shape of Howard Maddock's fish of 16lb 3ozs just 1oz over Pete Woodhouse's record. The fish was caught on the afternoon of Saturday, 29 November 1997, near Upton, and was witnessed by at least five experienced barbel anglers. It measured 32in × 19in in pristine condition. On the day of capture, the Severn was running some 14ft above normal!

This fish remained as the record until the following August (1998) when Stephen Keer, a teacher from Norwich caught a fish weighing 16lb 6oz from Taverham Mills weirpool on the river Wensum in Norfolk while fishing for chub.

REPEAT CAPTURE

The fish had been caught many times before by a number of anglers, including Stephen himself who had caught it at 15lb 6oz in September 1997.

Two other anglers, Andy Jubb and Andy Creasey both had the fish at the same weight (15lb 6oz) during September–October 1997.

Stephen's fish was the same one as that caught by David Livermore in September 1995 and measured 28in × 21½in looking more like a carp than a barbel. Despite Stephen stating that he would not be targeting the fish again, he recaptured it in August 1998 at 16lb 1oz. However, the situation was not going to remain the same for very long and in November 1998 an Ouse fish filled the top spot. Fishing in diabolical weather conditions of gales and torrential rain, Dave Currell of Borehamwood recorded a fish of 16lb 11oz from the Adams Mill stretch of the river. Having put off a trip to the river Severn due to severe conditions, he decided to head across to the Ouse where conditions were marginally better.

Getting thoroughly soaked to the skin after roving between swims, he was forced to sit it out under an umbrella. On the verge of packing up, he cast his flavoured Spam bait to the edge of a slack, away from the main force of the current. A strong pull on the rod top from a very large barbel resulted in the record being broken and history was made.

The fish measured 31in x 21¼in and was witnessed by fellow barbel angler, Ray Walton and Milton Keynes bailiff, Ben Ball who had turned out especially to assist in the weighing. The fish had been caught by a variety of anglers at lesser weights and it was no surprise when Dunstable expert, Martin Bowler recaptured it at 16lb 12oz on Tuesday, 21 January 1999. Conditions again were appalling, with the river covering an area a mile wide due to extensive flooding over the preceding days. Martin had to wade out through the water to be able to cast a line from a small grassy island. A boilie with paste wrapped around it was the successful bait, the fish being witnessed by Ray Walton and Guy Robb.

Only a fortnight later, the same fish fell yet again to Rainham Essex all-round specialist Kevin Newton, making him the first barbel angler to break the 17lb barrier at 17lb 1oz.

GREATEST ACHIEVEMENT

Perhaps the greatest achievement, however, was that of Ray Walton a month later (March 1999) when he landed the same fish at 17lb 4oz. This was after forty-one trips to the stretch for only one other barbel. The fish was caught in the afternoon from a slightly high and coloured river using his normal method of rolling Spam through the swim.

Despite intense angling pressure on the record-breaking stretch (Adams Mill/Kickles Farm) throughout the season, it wasn't until March 2000 that Guy Robb, fishing during an evening session and roving the banks after pre-baiting three favourite swims, had a bite in his final pre-baited swim. After a 10-minute scrap, his scales registered a new British record at 17lb 6oz 12dr. confirmed after the required scales check. Witnessed by pal, Stuart Morgan, and local barbel expert, Eric Frewin, the fish had fallen for a John Baker Search 4 paste bait.

To capture a record barbel is in itself a tremendous achievement, but to break the barbel record twice in nine days is spectacular to say the least.

December 2000 saw more heavy rain sweeping the country, and Chippenham, Wiltshire-based angler Stuart Morgan had already put off a trip to his local Bristol Avon due to excessive flooding. After checking the weather forecast, he realized that the rainfall in the Bedfordshire/Buckinghamshire areas surrounding the Great Ouse had been less torrential than elsewhere, so his first trip of the season to the Ouse took place on Tuesday, 5 December 2000.

The river was four feet up and had a temperature of 48°F (9°C) but Stuart's intention was not to fish but to pre-bait a number of swims away from known snags.

Stuart Morgan with the magnificent 17lb 9oz barbel caught in December 2000 in the Great Ouse. At the time this was the British barbel record. On the same day Stuart also caught another barbel, this second fish weighing in at 14lb 4oz.

Having achieved this, he made the 120-mile trip back to Wiltshire, returning the very next day at around 4pm to find the river had risen and was now carrying six feet of coloured floodwater. No other anglers were present – hardly surprising considering the gale and heavy rain conditions.

Needing 6oz of sea lead to hold bottom, a large barbel was hooked, but the fine wire no. 8 hook straightened out, allowing the fish to break free. This effectively killed off hopes of any more action that day. Three days later Stuart was again on the banks, but due to a combination of road accidents and heavy traffic he didn't arrive until 4pm after driving for 9½ hours! Continental boilie hooks were used this time, combined with 12lb main line and the usual 6oz crab lead. Bait was paste-wrapped around a mini cork ball. Thirty minutes later, a 17lb 9oz barbel graced his net, being witnessed by Len Gurd and Guy Robb. Another fish of 14lb 4oz was caught later in the session, making a brace total of 31lb 13oz – another UK record!

On 20 December 2000 he was back on the same bank, courtesy of a business meeting being held in the area. Arriving at 6pm, he found the river to be just two feet above normal, but the water temperature had dropped to 46°F (8°C). At around 7.30pm a sharp tug was followed by a solid resistance and, following a long fight, the scales registered 17lb 14oz – beating his own UK record set just days earlier. As it was so close to Christmas most people were engaged with parties or shopping activities, and it proved difficult to summon the required witnesses. However, the *Angling Times* staff responded and turned out to witness and photograph the catch.

Many anglers thought this would be the largest fish of the season (2000–01) as the weather had left extensive flooding right across the country and the forecast for early March was more of the same. But only a matter of days after Stuart's historical catch, the very first UK barbel of 19lb was recorded from the Great Ouse by Tony Gibson, an all-round specialist angler from

Northampton. Fishing a short evening session before attending a Northampton specimen group meeting, Tony lured the monster with a boilie/paste combination bait. The river was again in flood and rising, requiring a 4oz lead to hold bottom. It was landed on a 12ft Armalite rod with a 2¼lb test curve.

It remains doubtful that this fish is the one caught by Stuart, having added 1lb 2oz in weight in just a few days. There are thought to be around fifteen very large barbel in the 2-mile stretch, many over 15lb.

The season (2000–01) was brought to a premature end by the foot-and-mouth epidemic that swept across the country from February effectively closing both rivers and access fields into the foreseeable future.

The season 2001–02 opened on a far happier note, with many of the foot-and-mouth restrictions having been lifted, allowing access to many of the country's rivers. The spotlight again fell on the Great Ouse, with expectations that the first 20lb barbel would be caught before the end of the season. However, this was not to be, although Steve Curtin of Bedford increased the record to 19lb 6½oz with a memorable catch.

Fishing on 27 October 2001 on a river that was inches from bursting its banks, Steve landed the huge fish on his second cast using a John Baker boilie as bait. Just two hours later he landed a 14lb 9oz fish, making it the biggest barbel brace on record at 33lb 15½oz.

The season ended with a total of eight barbel being caught at over 18lb, including the record fish, with Tony Miles' fish at 19lb 2oz being the best of the rest. Many of the fish caught over the season on the Great Ouse had obviously been recaptures, and anglers expressed some concern that a 'known' barbel had lost several ounces in weight.

With these fish being in pristine condition it is anticipated that they have several growing years in front of them and, given time, will challenge the existing record. Estimating a potential weight for these fish in, say, three to five years, a conservative figure of 21–23lb would appear to be realistic.

There is no doubt that barbel are getting bigger across the country, with most rivers showing an increase of between 1–4lb compared to ten years ago. The Great Ouse is a unique river, but no one fully understands why it should produce barbel that are 4–5lb heavier than those of other UK rivers. Factors such as clean water and a large amount of natural and unnatural food (anglers' baits) together with little competition from other species such as chub and carp, have all contributed. A continuing influx of nitrates and phosphates running off the land into rivers, especially in flood conditions, have increased plant life and the associated invertebrates that barbel rely on.

Global warming has also added to the equation, producing a pattern of milder autumns and winters, allowing barbel to feed for longer sustainable periods due to the corresponding rise in water temperatures. For example, October 2001 was the warmest October since records began in the eighteenth century!

A heavy bombardment of highly nutritional baits such as boilies and pastes have also assisted barbel in increasing their weight in many rivers across the the country.

Whether we will be looking at record barbel in the 21–24lb class in a few years remains to be seen, but above all let's hope that our rivers remain clear and free-flowing and that our beloved barbel have many successful spawning years ahead – guaranteeing the enjoyment of future generations of anglers.

The UK's First 20lb Barbel
Tony Gibson's exclusive account of its capture

As we headed into October, it was time to get serious about catching a big barbel from 'The Mill'. It's often the first time following the start of the new season when we experience a sustained amount of wet weather. Extra water carrying additional colour can lead to some strong feeding spells and a certain reduction in the amount of caution displayed by the barbel. An added bonus is that by the start of October most fish are displaying a pleasing weight gain, with some fish really packing on a substantial amount in a comparatively short period of time. With all this in mind I planned two or three days off work each week over a two-week period. This would hopefully give me the chance to familiarize myself with the latest fish movements and also give me an idea of which swims were receiving pressure from either simply being fished, or from actual fish captures.

On the first week I had the Monday, Tuesday and Friday off work. This period resulted in a fish of 16lb 2oz. This was obviously a very pleasing result, but was also a great boost in helping to finalize on my bait and tactics for the remainder of my mini autumn campaign.

I was next down on the Sunday, with the prospect of the following two days off work. I'd narrowed swim choice down to two swims that I felt gave me the best chance of one of the huge barbel that I was really after. I fished my first-choice swim on the Sunday, keeping free offerings to a minimum, with only a small PVA mesh bag of mixed pellet and crumbled boilies tied to the lead on each cast. The day ended with no definite indications of interest from the barbel. I'd experienced a couple of tentative rod-top rattles, but these could easily have been the ever-present chub showing some interest.

The following day started wet and windy, much as it had been all night. Due to the inclement conditions and the fact that I'd only managed to snatch a couple of hours' sleep, I had a bit of a lie-in and didn't arrive at the fishery until around 08.45. Despite the late start I still had the whole fishery to myself and therefore decided to stick with my first-choice swim.

My tackle consisted of one of the rods from the Bob Church stable that bears my name, teamed up with an old Shimano 'baitrunner' loaded with 10lb Fox monofilament. The hooklength comprised of a combi-link of around 2½ft of 12lb fluorocarbon tied via a five-turn water knot to approximately 2in of 10lb 'Edge' braid that terminated in a strong size 10 'Big T' hook. As the river had risen by a good few inches (and was still rising) from the previous day, I increased the size of the Pallatrax 'Stonze' ledger weight to ensure the end-tackle stayed where I wanted it. To keep the mainline above the end-tackle pinned to the deck, a semi-fixed back-lead was incorporated into the set-up approximately 1½ft up from the main ledger weight. An additional sliding back-lead was used to keep the bulk of the mainline snug to the river bed; this was slid down the mainline following the cast.

Although the conditions looked very favourable all day, as we headed toward the last hour or so, no barbel had been landed either by me or by the two other members who had arrived later that morning. Eventually it was time to take the final cast of the day. I'd swapped the hookbait from a single 15mm 'Source' boilie to two 10mm boilies of the same type and also used a tiny PVA mesh bag of pellet tied to the lead, together with a small stringer of two whole and two halved 10mm boilies tied to the hook next to the hair-rigged hookbait. Once the rod was in the rests and everything settled, it was time to sit back and wait.

continued overleaf

Tony Gibson's historic capture – the country's first-ever 20lb barbel. No wonder he's smiling!

Time was running out, but as I stepped toward the rod to finally wind in, the tip suddenly lurched over as a barbel finally made a mistake. Fortunately there were no particular fireworks on the fish's part, just a slow, but strong and steady, plod around the swim, indicating that a big fish had been hooked. As it eventually neared the net, the fish made a couple of lunges in the direction of a nearby reed bed. However everything held firm and the fish was steered over the outstretched landing net.

Looking into the net I was able to confirm what I had already started to suspect. There in my landing net lay the barbel I'd most wanted to catch … 'Traveller'! As Stuart, the only other member left on-site, looked after the net and fish I quickly got the mat and weighing gear together. We both knew that I could easily have a new PB to hold up for the cameras, but also realized that there was a chance that 'Traveller' could surpass the current record. However, I was totally unprepared for what happened next. As Stuart steadied himself and carefully held up the scales the needle spun around to show a weight of 20lb 6oz! I initially had a problem in believing what my eyes were telling me, so we went through the weighing procedure again, this time with me holding the scales and Stuart calling off the weight. Yes, no doubt, 20lb 6oz it was!

Time to get the mobile out and make some calls!

Barbel Record Holders – Past and Present as at 15 March 2004

Weight lb oz	Captor	Location	Month/Year
20 06	Tony Gibson	Great Ouse	Oct 2004
19 06½	Steve Curtin	Great Ouse	Oct 2001
19 00	Tony Gibson	Great Ouse	Jan 2001
17 14	Stuart Morgan	Great Ouse	Dec 2000
17 09	Stuart Morgan	Great Ouse	Dec 2000
17 06¾	Guy Robb	Great Ouse	Mar 2000
17 04	Ray Walton	Great Ouse	Mar 1999
17 01	Kevin Newton	Great Ouse	Feb 1999
16 12	Martin Bowler	Great Ouse	Jan 1999
16 11	Dave Currell	Great Ouse	Nov 1998
16 06	Stephen Keer	Wensum	Aug 1998
16 03	Howard Maddocks	Severn	Nov 1997
16 02	Pete Woodhouse	Medway	Jun 1994
15 11	Andy Harman	Medway	Sept 1993
15 07	Bob Morris	Medway	Jan 1993
14 13	David Taylor	Medway	Nov 1992
14 09	David Taylor	Medway	Nov 1992
14 06½	David Williams	Hants Avon	Sept 1992
14 06	David Williams	Medway	Sept 1992
14 06**	Hon. Aylmer Tyron	Hants Avon	Sept 1934
14 06	F.W.K. Wallis	Hants Avon	Sept 1937
14 06	T. Wheeler	Thames	1888

**Note: Tyron's fish reinstated as UK Record in August 1990 after being dropped from the list in 1968, along with joint record holders of the time.

Note:

13 12	Joe Day	Hants Avon	Oct 1962

This fish replaced Tyron/Wallis/Wheeler's fish in 1968 as the UK record barbel but anglers across the country chose to recognize Tyron's fish at 14lb 6oz as the one to beat.

During this confusion the fish caught at 14lb 2oz by Martin Hooper in the Dorset Stour in September 1987 was awarded interim record status when, in January 1990, he was encouraged by the angling media to submit a retrospective record claim.

Rejected Records Claims 1990–2004 – Barbel

Weight lb oz	Captor	Location	Month/Year
15 12	Jason Bailey	Wey (Surrey)	Aug 1990
16 05	Ray Wood	Great Ouse	July 1997
16 13	John Fulton	Wensum	Oct 1998
17 10	Trevor Wilson	Great Ouse	Mar 2000

Note: If the above fish had been accepted by the BRFC they would have become the largest barbel caught in the country at the time.

Jason Bailey – Wey – 15lb 12oz, August 1990

Surrey teenager Jason Bailey reported a brace of barbel to the angling press at weights of 15lb and 13lb both caught in July 1990 from the river Wey in Surrey. Doubts were cast on the weights claimed so Jason set out to prove the river's potential.

Fishing at Waltham Lock on a private stretch, the Pyrford angler caught a huge barbel of 15lb 12oz during August 1990, using a Diawa Heavy Feeder rod with Maxima 8lb main line and sausage meat as bait. The fish measured 36½in to the tip of its tail having a girth of 23in, both measurements consistent with a fish of this weight.

Although photographs were published in the weekly press with Jason holding the fish, doubts were again cast on the weight claimed. As Jason had correctly submitted his claim and had followed the required guidelines laid down by the BRFC (British Rod Caught Fish Committee), it came as a surprise that they chose initially to reject the claim, later freezing his submission pending further investigation in January 1991.

Expert barbel anglers Ray Walton and Fred Crouch took up Jason's case and there was much debate concerning this, when, during NASA's (National Association of Specialist Anglers) Annual Conference at Loughborough University in February 1991, a furious row broke out in the Main Hall. BRFC officials present dismissed suggestions that the claim had not been favourably received because the angler was an 'unknown' name. No reasons were provided by the BRFC when, in November 1991, the fish was finally rejected. Surprisingly, the two independent witnesses, Kevin de Dench-Layton and Jacqueline Adams from Woking, were never contacted in order to substantiate Jason's claim. This led to cries for a fresh Code of Adjudication to be introduced, especially as the BRFC Handbook stated that: 'Claims are considered and adjudicated upon, only on the basis that the Committee shall be under no obligation whatsoever to claimants, that its decisions shall be final, and it shall not be obliged to give reason for its decisions.' A very unsatisfactory situation, especially as a full statement was never issued to the angling press.

Ray Wood – Great Ouse – 16lb 5oz, July 1997

It was thought that the British barbel record had been smashed with a 16lb 5oz fish from the Great Ouse in July 1997. Its captor, Ray Wood of East Ham, London had been targeting the river above Bedford from the start of the season and news of his huge fish filtered through to the angling press. However, Ray decided not to submit a record claim stating that he did not want to increase angling pressure on the stretch. This stance caused the angling press to go into 'overdrive' with letters being printed every week, mostly appealing to Ray to publish a photograph of the fish for the country's historical records.

With the various barbel groups entering the fray the whole matter was starting to get out of hand, resulting in Ray having to use the services of a solicitor to defend his position. Certainly this was an extraordinary course of action to take.

Although claims were made that a photograph did exist, this was never presented to the angling press, nor were any witnesses ever produced. The whole issue lacked authenticity and several accusations were alleged to have been made that the whole episode had been manufactured in order to snub a fellow angler! – a terrible state of affairs. In hindsight, a 16lb barbel from the Great Ouse hardly raises an eyebrow nowadays (2004).

John Fulton – River Wensum – 16lb 13oz, October 1998

While watching John Wilson on Sky TV during one of his fishing programmes, John Fulton from Friern Barnet, London, decided to take a fishing break in Norfolk staying at the holiday complex at Taverham Mill near Norwich.

Being a carp angler, his attention had previously been centred on them until he decided he wanted to catch his first-ever barbel.

Having borrowed suitable barbel gear from a friend because his heavy carp gear was totally unsuitable, he tackled the mill pool with a lobworm on a size 6 hook, using a dough bobbin as an indicator. When the bobbin started to rise, he thought that the current was responsible, but, having pushed it downwards, it flew up to smack the rod.

After a spirited fight he landed the fish, which was recognized as 'Red Belly' (not to be confused with the Great Ouse resident) and registered a weight of 16lb 14oz on the scales. A later test carried out on the scales by Peterborough City Council Weights and Measures office revealed that the 'avons' were showing 1oz heavy.

Later feedback indicated that the fish had been weighed in a plastic bag that may have contained water. With the weighing evidence in doubt the fish never entered the record books.

Trevor Wilson – Great Ouse – 17lb 10oz, March 2000

Switching from his regular river Kennet, Trevor, who comes from Walton-on-Thames, Surrey, decided on a late-season session on the Adams Mill stretch of the Great Ouse with his angling colleague Graeme Attwood. Both anglers had fished the river since 1999 achieving fourteen double-figure barbel between them, the best at 16lb 10oz.

Having started on the river in the morning, Trevor had the choice of one of the 'good swims' and after just one hour hooked into a fish that immediately snagged him on the far bank. He decided to wade out in the freezing water that came up to his chestwaders and managed to free the fish that registered 13lb 14oz.

At around 4pm, having sat for a number of hours in his soaking clothing, he struck into another large fish that immediately headed for the same snag. Having tried every angle in an attempt to free the fish he decided that no matter how big the fish was, its welfare came first and with that in mind he passed his rod to Graeme with the fish still attached. He then went round to the far bank with another rod. From there he cast across to Graeme with the aid of a small weight. He tied the line to the reel and wound the whole lot across the river.

He was then able to free the fish with his original rod and finally land it. The whole operation took about twenty-five minutes. It was accurately weighed on two sets of Avon Dial scales that read 17lb 10oz and was witnessed by four different anglers.

When considering any potential record claim the BRFC have to consider their laid-down procedures, one of which is that the angler must have solely lured, played and caught the fish in order to claim a national record.

Trevor commented in October 2000 that he 'didn't think it would be accepted' because of the circumstances surrounding its capture. Trevor, a special effects model-maker, has caught over 200 double-figure barbel and primarily fishes for fun. He did not really want to submit a record claim in the first place but with the media spotlight on the fish, he was persuaded into it.

The fish was recognized as 'Red Belly', being the best one of the four 16lb fish caught by Ouse local John Barford at 16lb 15oz in January 2000. The same fish that

Steve Curtin recorded at 19lb 6½oz in October 2001 and later found dead on the banks of the river at the end of September 2002 at a weight of 19lb 8oz. If accepted, the fish would have beaten Guy Robb's Great Ouse record fish of 17lb 6¾oz caught earlier in March 2000. Trevor's concern for the welfare of the fish may have cost him a place in the record books.

BEST BARBEL BRACES
AS AT 16 JUNE 2004

In compiling a list of barbel braces, defined as two fish caught in the same day, it is noticeable that the Great Ouse dominates the picture, with the vast majority of fish coming from this one river. Only the Medway in its heyday, and more recently,

the Dorset Stour, have produced fish to challenge it.

Compared to some ten years ago, almost all the country's rivers are now producing barbel some 1–4lb heavier, with the Ouse being a unique case in that its fish are now 6–7lb heavier than those caught in the early 1990s. Various reasons have been put forward as to why this has occurred nationally, among which are: global warming, more anglers' high-protein baits, excellent water quality and milder autumns and winters, allowing the barbel to feed for longer sustainable periods.

The result is that at the end of each season (late February/March), expectations run high concerning the Great Ouse and its ability to produce the country's first 20lb barbel. With a handful of known fish with the capacity to put on the required weight, this remains a strong possibility,

Best Barbel Braces (Two Fish in Same Day)
Top 20 revised as at 16 June 2004

Captor	Date	River	First fish lb oz		Second fish lb oz		Total lb oz	
Steve Curtin	Oct 2001	Gt Ouse	19	06½	14	09	33	15½
Stuart Morgan	Dec 2000	Gt Ouse	17	09	14	04	31	13
Trevor Wilson	Mar 2000	Gt Ouse	17	10	13	14	31	08
Graeme Attwood	Mar 2000	Gt Ouse	15	10	15	09	31	03
Ray Walton	Mar 2003	Gt Ouse	17	12	12	15	30	11
Grahame King	Feb 2004	Gt Ouse	16	00	14	06	30	06
Ray Walton	Feb 2002	Gt Ouse	15	09	14	12	30	05
Guy Robb	Mar 1999	Gt Ouse	15	04	15	00	30	04
Adrian Busby	Nov 2002	Gt Ouse	15	04	14	12	30	00
Graeme Attwood	July 2000	Gt Ouse	15	04	14	09	29	13
Ray Walton	Mar 2003	Gt Ouse	17	03	12	09	29	12
Mark Ward	June 2003	Gt Ouse	13	07	16	04	29	11
Martin Bowler	Sept 1998	Gt Ouse	15	06	14	03	29	09
Dave Charles	Mar 2003	Dorset Stour	15	01	14	02	29	03
Adrian Busby	June 1999	Gt Ouse	15	00	14	00	29	00
Stef Horak	Sept 1998	Gt Ouse	13	12	15	04	29	00
Grahame King	Nov 2002	Gt Ouse	14	06	14	04	28	10
Dave Williams	Nov 1994	Medway	13	03	15	03	28	06
Chris Turnbull	2002–03	Wensum	15	03	13	02	28	05
Richard Wallis	Oct 2003	Kennet	16	03	12	01	28	04

certainly within the next three years when we could be looking at barbel in the 21–22lb class. Admittedly, it is difficult to imagine Steve Curtin's wonderful brace of barbel being beaten, but, as they say, anything is possible.

Steve Curtin – Great Ouse – Saturday, 27 October 2001

First fish	19lb 6½oz
Second fish	14lb 9oz
Total weight	33lb 15½oz

Steve Curtin will never forget his fishing trip on 27 October 2001. Normally, only having the opportunity to fish on Sundays, he decided to switch days, ending up on the banks of the Great Ouse, above Bedford. The rest, as they say, is history.

His decision was based on the fact that heavy rain had fallen during the week and he wanted to take advantage of the extra water on the river before it fell back. Arriving at 11.30am he viewed the river that was just inches away from bursting its banks. He chose a fast smooth glide that followed a nice-looking bend to tackle up with a Hexagraph 11ft × 1½lb Avon rod, 10lb Diawa line, a 25-year-old ABU Cardinal 55reel, and a 1½oz lead weight. Bait was a John Baker boilie with his own paste bait used as a wrap.

Using PVA stringers he made five casts. On the sixth cast, he eventually located the gravel that he wanted and settled down to await events. Some twenty minutes later the rod top gave a 6in pull. This was followed by a stronger pull that kept on going. The fish shot to the far bank in

The fish looks happy too! Steve Curtin with the 14lb 9oz barbel he caught on the Great Ouse on 27 October 2001, just two hours after he had caught the British record fish weighing 19lb 6oz 8dr.

the fast current, but Steve managed, after much pulling, to get it over to his own bank, where it tried to get into the rushes at his feet. After coaxing the fish to the surface, it dived a couple more times before ending up in the large triangular landing net.

Friends Dick and Mel helped with the weighing procedures. After zeroing the 40lb Avon scales, the needle registered 19lb 6½oz, a new British barbel record. A further check was made on a separate set of scales with the same result.

Feeling slightly dazed by the whole episode, Steve decided on another cast and, two hours later, another bite resulted in a 14lb 9oz barbel, making it a new best barbel brace record for two fish caught in one session. What a day! The water temperature had been 53°F, air pressure down from 1017 to 1012, and it was later confirmed that October 2001 had been the warmest October since records began back in the 1800s.

Stuart Morgan – Great Ouse – 9 December 2000

First fish	17lb 9oz
Second fish	14lb 4oz
Total weight	31lb 13oz

After spending some nine hours in traffic, travelling from his Wiltshire home, Stuart could easily have abandoned the idea of fishing for large barbel, especially when viewing the swollen river that was bank high and running a strange orange-brown colour. However, he persevered with a number of leads, finally having to settle on a 6oz watch lead just to hold bottom, in conjunction with a 12lb main line.

After some thirty minutes, he retrieved the John Baker paste bait, dropping a fresh offering a few feet from the bank in fairly fast water. The rod tip dipped and

juddered almost immediately, the resulting strike being met with solid resistance from a very large barbel.

Initially the fish charged off into the main flow, twisting and turning just below the surface, putting a huge strain on Stuart's 12ft Insight rod, before he could scramble down the bank to net the fish. Carefully lifting the fish out, the scales registered 17lb 10oz, later reduced to 17lb 9oz after the obligatory trading standards weight check. This was a new British barbel record, beating Guy Robb's 17lb 6oz March 2000 record.

Having been witnessed by Len Gurd and Guy Robb, the fish was returned safely, allowing time for one more cast. A strong bite produced a second barbel of 14lb 4oz – at the time of capture the largest brace of barbel ever caught. With Stuart's emphasis on the welfare of this fish, it was returned safely before everyone realized that no photographs had been taken!

Trevor Wilson – Great Ouse – March 2000

First fish	17lb 10oz
Second fish	13lb 14oz
Total weight	31lb 8oz

Note: First fish rejected for record claim – see separate section

Graeme Attwood – Great Ouse – 15 March 2000

First fish	15lb 9oz
Second fish	15lb 10oz
Total weight	31lb 3oz

Fishing on the last day of the 1999–2000 season, Graeme arrived at Kickles Farm around 7am on a very mild day. After pre-baiting with some boilies, he had only fifteen minutes to wait before his Guy Robb Barbel Quiver Rod pulled round, the heavy fish making short determined runs before being netted. It weighed a colossal 15lb 9oz.

It remained quiet until 3pm when a large barbel ran into a far bank snag: after becoming free it was safely netted recording a weight of 15lb 10oz making it an incredible 31lb 3oz for just two fish, the fourth best brace ever recorded.

The session ended just before 6pm with an 11lb 4oz fish. The fish were witnessed by Adrian Busby. Bait was Graeme's own protein mix with J.B. Frost and Flood flavour added. Fireline Mainline matched to a Snakebite hook link completed the picture.

Ray Walton – Great Ouse – March 2003

First fish	17lb 12oz
Second fish	12lb 15oz
Total weight	30lb 11oz

The water levels on the Great Ouse were lower than normal in the last few weeks of the season (2002–03) resulting in fewer large barbel being caught than expected. Ray Walton, however, persisted with his rolling meat method. Using large chunks of luncheon meat (Spam), he eventually struck lucky with a huge 17lb 12oz fish, following this up with a 12lb 15oz barbel a few hours later.

Ray, a previous barbel record holder, stated that it had been a tough end to the season, with the river in poor shape.

The brace of fish gave a total of 30lb 11oz making it the third largest brace ever caught at the time. A few days later he landed a 15lb 14oz fish, making him the most successful angler on the river during that season. The tackle used was a Harrison 1lb 3oz TC 11ft River

Roller rod with 30lb Spiderwire main line.

Grahame King – Great Ouse – February 2004

First fish	16lb
Second fish	14lb 6ozs
Total weight	30lb 6ozs

Taking advantage of a mild spell, Grahame reached his half-century of double-figure barbel with a 16lb specimen followed by a 14lb 6oz, two hours later. Both fish fell for John Baker paste and boilies. A previous session had resulted in a 15lb 8oz fish.

Ray Walton – Great Ouse – February 2002

First fish	15lb 9oz
Second fish	14lb 12oz
Total weight	30lb 5oz

Toward the end of the season 2001–02 many anglers on the Great Ouse were failing to locate any of the river's huge barbel. One angler who did succeed however, was previous barbel record holder, Ray Walton, with a run of five 'doubles'.

The highlight was a brace of barbel weighing a total of 30lb 5oz. First to the net was a huge fish of 15lb 9oz, followed within an hour by another of 14lb 12oz.

Bournemouth-based Ray used his favoured rolling meat method. The other specimens weighed in at 14lb 6oz, 13lb 12oz and 10lb 2oz.

Guy Robb – Great Ouse – Saturday, 13th March 1999

First fish	15lb 4oz
Second fish	15lb
Total weight	30lb 4oz

The last few days of the 1998–99 season saw Guy on the banks of the Great Ouse. Having pre-baited the day before on a lightly fished stretch known to contain a few very large barbel, he returned on the Saturday. His very first cast with a hair-rigged John Baker paste, attached to 10lb Big Game line and a size 8 hook, produced an instant response from a 15lb 4oz barbel. Flushed with success, Guy decided to pull off the river for an early lunch in Milton Keynes, returning a few hours later.

His second cast of the day, six hours after the first one, produced a strong fish that powered off downstream. The scales recorded 15lb exactly. It was an incredible feat of angling: in just two casts he had two fish totalling 30lb 4oz, which is presently the eighth best barbel brace of all time, but at the time of capture it represented the biggest brace of barbel ever recorded in the UK. This feat won Guy a Drennan Cup award.

Adrian Busby – Great Ouse – November 2002

First fish	15lb 4oz
Second fish	14lb 12oz
Total weight	30lb

Corn-lover Adrian Busby was experimenting with high nutritional value baits when he enjoyed success with a brace of barbel from the Great Ouse. The fish weighed in at 15lb 4oz and 14lb 12oz.

They both took Mike Willmott's Essential Products Big Barbel Mix paste on a

A remarkable day's fishing. Graeme Attwood with a 15lb 4oz barbel that he caught on the Great Ouse in July 2000. On the same day, Graeme also caught barbel weighing 11lb 15oz, 14lb 9oz and 7lb 9oz.

stiff link rig with a size 8 hook to 12lb main line. Firefighter Adrian won a Fox award for his capture.

Graeme Attwood – Great Ouse – July 2000

First fish	14lb 9oz
Second fish	15lb 4oz
Total weight	29lb 13oz

Tackling the Adam's Mill stretch on a drizzly July day, Graeme had no inkling of the sequence of events about to unfold. Starting around 2pm a barbel of 11lb 15oz came to the net, falling for the cinnamon spice-flavoured bait. Later in the afternoon, a larger fish of 14lb 9oz found the bait irresistible, becoming the subject of a photo session with both Trevor Wilson and Bob Church in attendance.

The action was far from over as a 7lb 9oz barbel was banked, and with the rain now getting heavier, Graeme's 'bottom' rod was pulled round, this time a huge fish of 15lb 4oz appearing in the bottom of the landing net. The two larger fish made it an historical 'barbel brace' of 29lb 13oz. This gave Graeme the tenth best brace on record. Tackle was Bruce Ashby Quiver Rods matched to 14lb Fireline main line.

Ray Walton – Great Ouse – March 2003

First fish	17lb 3oz
Second fish	12lb 9oz
Total weight	29lb 12oz

Former record holder and Barbel Specialists founder, Ray Walton, concentrated on the Great Ouse during the last few days of the 2002–03 season.

Ray from Dorset, again rolled Spam using an 11lb 3oz Harrison River Roller rod, together with a size 2 Drennan Boilie Hook to 30lb Spiderwire, banking a 17lb 3oz and 12lb 9oz barbel in the same session, making it one of the largest braces on record.

Mark Ward holds 'The Traveller' that he caught on the Great Ouse on 21 June 2003. The fish weighed 16lb 4oz. Earlier in the day Mark had landed a barbel weighing 13lb 7oz.

Mark Ward – Great Ouse – 20 June 2003

First fish	13lb 7oz
Second fish	16lb 4oz
Total weight	29lb 11oz

Mark 'kicked off' his barbel season in great style, fishing short sessions during June/July on the syndicate stretch of the Great Ouse at Newport Pagnell.

Using just one rod, a Graham Phillips 11ft × 1¼ TC and 12lb Big Game line, he equalled his personal best with a fish of 13lb 7oz late in the evening of 20 June, the fish falling for a 12mm boilie wrapped in paste.

Around two hours later he landed 'The Traveller' at 16lb 4oz making a brace of 29lb 11oz. This fish was caught again by Stuart Court in September 2003 at 19lb 2oz and is easily recognizable with its split lower tail. Over just a few weeks, Mark took an eight-fish catch, including other fish of 9lb 12oz, 9lb 15oz, 10lb 12oz, 15lb 4oz and 15lb 6oz.

Martin Bowler – Great Ouse – September 1998

First fish	15lb 6oz
Second fish	14lb 3oz
Total weight	29lb 9oz

Dispensing with the idea of going bream fishing, Martin instead decided to set off for the Great Ouse to target its large barbel. The day started without a cloud in the sky, promising to be a very hot one. Armed only with a pair of polaroids, Martin strolled along the banks looking for fish. He noticed that the river was running low and clear, not ideal conditions for big whiskers.

Arriving at a large overhanging tree where the water deepened, he noticed the tail of a large barbel sticking out

from under some streamer weed. After groundbaiting with maggot and hemp, everything was left to settle for an hour or two before he cast in a mini-boilie covered in John Baker paste close to the overhanging tree. It wasn't long before the 12ft × 1½ TC Harrison rod was wrenched from its rod rest, with all hell being let loose!

His priority was to stop the fish from going back under the overhanging branches and maximum pressure was applied to the 10lb line. Some five minutes later a pristine barbel was lying in the net. The scales told the truth at 15lb 6oz – a fish that had previously been caught by both Stef Horak and Pete Reading.

Events were repeated a short time later. This time the fish weighed 14lb 3oz, giving a brace total of 29lb 9oz, thereby beating Stef Horak's best barbel brace of 29lb caught just two weeks earlier. Martin picked up a Shimano Specimen Cup award for his captures.

Dave Charles – Dorset Stour – March 2003

First fish	15lb 1oz
Second fish	14lb 2oz
Total weight	29lb 3oz

Making the best of the last few days of the 2002–03 season, Dave Charles a dairy farm manager from Ecchinswell, near Newbury, travelled down to the middle reaches of the Dorset Stour, targeting the river's big barbel.

During a day-long session, he caught the biggest brace of barbel ever taken from a river other than the Great Ouse, – the first fish being a monster of 15lb 1oz.

Witnessed by fellow barbel enthusiast Steve Derby from Sheffield, and weighed on two sets of scales, it was quickly followed by a fish of 14lb 2oz. Both fish fell for

The fish known as 'The Pope' is proudly held before the camera by Adrian Busby. The fish was caught on the Great Ouse in June 1999 and Adrian also landed a second fish, this one weighing 14lb, in the same session.

garlic-flavoured HNV paste/boilie combinations, together with a PVA stringer. Tackle comprised a 12ft 1lb 4oz Kev Baynes Specialist rod, Stanton centrepin reel and 10lb Big Game line. A Kamasan size 8 River Carp hook completed the picture.

Dave won a Kevlar Fox Multi Tip rod donated by the *Coarse Angling Today* magazine.

Adrian Busby – Great Ouse – June 1999

First fish	15lb
Second fish	14lb
Total weight	29lb

Using ledgered sweetcorn, Adrian caught the fish known as 'The Pope' at 15lb from the Great Ouse 'somewhere above Bedford'. Adrian's second fish, weighing 14lb, was recognized as the same fish he had caught in July 1994 at just 11lb 7oz, which was his very first double-figure barbel from Adam's Mill.

Although Adrian loves to refer to this fish as Sail, because it had the habit of extending its dorsal fin as soon as a photograph was taken, it later became known as 'Red Belly' falling to Steve Curtin's rod in October 2001. Unfortunately, this fish was found dead in the river in September 2002.

Stef Horak – Great Ouse – September 1998

First fish	13lb 12oz
Second fish	15lb 4oz
Total weight	29lb

Big fish ace Stef Horak bagged what was, at the time, the biggest brace of barbel on record, in just two casts on the Great Ouse. Casting close to weed beds, Stef, from Stoney Stanton in Leicestershire, took both fish from a stretch of the river 'above Bedford'.

After hours of stalking and baiting up a variety of swims with sweetcorn and hemp, he used his maggot feeder to great effect, with the first fish weighing a respectable 13lb 12oz. The second fish exceeded his expectations, bringing the scales round to 15lb 4oz.

The capture gave Stef a Drennan Cup weekly award and completed a four-day stint that also took in the Hampshire Avon and that produced chub of 5lb 5oz and 5lb 4oz.

Grahame King – Great Ouse – November 2002

First fish	14lb 6oz
Second fish	14lb 4oz
Total weight	28lb 10oz

After a fishing trip to Costa Rica, Grahame King decided to return to the Great Ouse in pursuit of the large barbel that reside 'above Bedford'. The Watford-based angler scaled down his tackle to keep in touch with the fish, this approach proving successful with a brace of barbel totalling 28lb 10oz.

The first barbel weighed 14lb 6oz and fell for a tiny piece of luncheon meat. He followed this up with a 14lb 4oz fish after switching to John Baker boilies.

The 14lb 6oz fish represented his twenty-fifth double of the season and, later in the session, he added another barbel of 13lb 12oz.

Dave Williams – Medway, Kent – 23 November 1994

First fish	13lb 3oz
Second fish	15lb 3oz
Total weight	28lb 6oz

With low air pressure accompanied by high winds and rain, Dave Williams from Bexley Heath, tackled his local river Medway at Fordcombe, knowing that such conditions often produced large barbel.

Intending to fish a short evening session, he persevered with the poor conditions, being rewarded at about 10.30pm with a fish of 13lb 3oz that fell for his paste bait fished on a size 6 hook.

Despite nearly falling in twice and having his brolly whisked away in the wind, he continued fishing and, on the stroke of midnight, his rod arched over again, resulting in a spirited fight from a barbel of 15lb 3oz.

Dave was forced to sack both fish until first light when he had the opportunity to find someone with a camera. It was thought that the 15lb 3oz fish was the same as the one caught by Sam Fox in September 1994 at a weight of 15lb 6oz.

The 15-pounder provided Dave with his seventh fish over 14lb and, along with the 13-pounder, represented the biggest brace ever caught in this country.

Chris Turnbull – Wensum – 2002–03

First fish	15lb 3oz
Second fish	13lb 2oz
Total weight	28lb 5oz

Another fish at 13lb 1oz in the same session (Source – Tim Ellis 14/1/04)

Richard Wallis – Kennet – October 2003

First fish	16lb 3oz
Second fish	12lb 1oz
Total weight	28lb 4oz

Ex-matchman Richard Wallis of Chiseldon had an amazing brace of big barbel after pre-baiting the stretch regularly with boilies and pellets. His first fish at 16lbs 3ozs fell for a frozen ready-made boilie near a known snag and put up a spirited scrap. Earlier in the season he caught a 15lb 9oz fish that was his personal best at the time. All fish were caught using a size 6 hook and 15lb hook length.

BARBEL UK RIVER RECORDS – STORIES OF GREAT CAPTURES AS AT 16 JUNE 2004

Anker (Staffs)

Weight	Captor	Date
10lb 2oz	Sean Allison	Sept 2003
9lb 6oz	John Turner	Sept 2003
9lb 4oz	John Turner	Sept 2003

Rising in North Warwickshire the river is a tributary of the river Tame. It flows through the towns of Nuneaton and Atherstone and on through the village of Polesworth into the county of Staffordshire before entering the town of Tamworth. The town stretch here flows through the castle grounds and ends at Ladybridge where it flows into the Tame.

Pioneering work by Sean Allison and friend John Turner produced some excellent barbel around September/October 2003 after tracking a small number of large barbel over several weeks. The river fishes best in high-water conditions – potential weight 11–12lb in two years.

Arun (Sussex)

Weight	Captor	Date
11lb 2oz	Brian Ayling	Nov 2003

This is a fast flowing river that joins the sea at Littlehampton. The higher reaches around Pulborough have habitat suitable for barbel to spawn in, but evidence of successful spawning years remains scarce.

A few barbel up to 8lb were distributed into Sussex rivers in 1974 involving around 80 fish and in 1995, 500 fish (4in × 8in) were released at Pulborough and 750 around New Bridge, Billinghurst.

Fishing the tidal part of the river in November 2003, specialist Brian Ayling tempted a barbel of 11lb 2oz on 18mm mussel boilies and Snakebite Gold Hook length. With reports of double-figure barbel being extremely rare from any of the Sussex rivers (Arun, Rother, Ouse and Uck), it is difficult to predict the potential of any of these rivers.

In the summer of 2003, a six-mile stretch suffered with a discharge of agricultural pesticide wiping out hundreds of fish.

Arrow (Warwickshire)

Weight	Captor	Date
11lb 1oz	John Heath	Nov 1996

Potential 2/3 years	12lb

This is a very small tributary of the Warwickshire Avon approximately 6 miles long. It rises north-east of Redditch running in a north/south direction joining the main river (Avon) near Alchester at the junction of the river Alne. Ref. *Regional Guide*, 1979, p. 164.

Having blanked on a salmon trip to Canada, John Heath from Selly Oak had a premonition that he would capture a large barbel from the Arrow. He promptly did

Barbel UK River Records as at 16 June 2004

	River	Weight lb oz	Date	Captor	Potential Weight lb
1	Anker (Staffs)	10 02	Sept 2003	Sean Allison	11
2	Arun (Sussex)	11 02	Nov 2003	Brian Ayling	12
3	Arrow (Warks)	11 01	Nov 1996	John Heath	12
4	Avon (Bristol)	15 09½	Feb 1998	Stuart Morgan	17
5	Avon (Hampshire)	15 01	Aug 2001	Jim Eggleton	17
6	Avon (Warks)	15 03	Mar 2004	Alan King	16
7	Blackwater (Berks)	11 04	Aug 1999	Bob Vince	12
8	Cherwell (Oxon)	13 00	Oct 2002	Mick Coleman	14
9	Colne (Middlesex)	15 05	Jan 2002	Paul Jebb	16
10	Colnebrook	8 01	Oct 1991	Andy Harman	10
11	Coppermill Stream	11 06	Oct 1992	David Poole	12
12	Dane (Cheshire)	14 04	Aug 1994	Phil Booth	15
13	Derwent (Derbys)	12 11	Nov 2003	Jamie Alexander	14
14	Derwent (Yorks)	12 06	Sept 1989	Jon Wolfe	13
15	Don (Yorks)	8 04	Sept 2002	Christian Lawrence	10
16	Dove (Staffs)	14 15	Mar 2003	–	16
17	Drapers Osier Bed	7 02	Aug 2000	Jim Knight	9
18	Ember (Surrey)	9 04	Aug 2001	Seb Pizzuto	11
19	Frome (Somerset)	10 15	Aug 1995	Andy Cowley	13
20	Holybrook	13 04	Oct 2003	Trevor King	14
21	Ivel (Beds)	13 02	Mar 2004	Keith Smith	16
22	Kennet (Berks)	16 10	Feb 2002	Edward Barder	18
23	Lea	15 00½	Mar 2002	Jason Shaw	16
24	Leam (Warks)	11 09	Mar 2000	Trevor Kennedy	12
25	Loddon (Berks)	15 15	Oct 2002	Paul West	17
26	Lugg (Hereford)	10 08	July 1999	Darren Godsall	11
27	Mease (Staffs)	13 00	Nov 1996	Phil Hart	14
28	Medway (Kent)	16 02	June 1994	Pete Woodhouse	17
29	Mole (Surrey)	13 05	Jan 2004	Paul Starkey	15
30	Nene (Northants)	13 00	Summer 2002	Duncan Kay	14
31	Nidd (Yorks)	11 04	Oct 1993	Phil Johnson	12
32	Ouse, Great*	19 06½	Oct 2001	Steve Curtin	21
33	Ouse (Sussex)	11 08½	Oct 2000	Kevin Colston Iles	12
34	Ouse (Yorks)	10 10	Sept 1998	John McNulty	12
35	Potts Stream (Oxon)	13 08	Oct 1968	John Ginifer	–
36	Ribble (Lancs)	14 07	Mar 2002	Mark Halstead	16
37	Rother (Sussex)	12 12	Jan 2004	Pete Foster	14
38	St Patricks Stream	15 08	Oct 2001	Keith Evans	16
39	Severn	16 03	Nov 1997	Howard Maddocks	18
40	Soar (Leics)	10 10	Feb 2002	Tony Swann	12
41	Sow (Staffs)	10 00½	Sept 2002	Stewart Bloor	11

	River	Weight lb oz	Date	Captor	Potential Weight lb
42	Stour (Dorset)	16 02	Feb 2003	Graham Sale	17
43	Stour (Kent)	9 06	June 2002	Carl Allman	10
44	Stour (Warks)	8 06	1989	Nick Palmer	10
45	Swale (Yorks)	12 12½	Oct 1991	Brian Barton	14
46	Taff (Wales)	14 08	Aug 2003	Justin Henwood	15
47	Teme	14 02	June 1994	Martin Bluck	15
48	Thame	9 12	2001	John Sheldon	10
49	Thames	14 13	Feb 2003	Ted Bryan	16
50	Trent	15 02	Feb 2004	Tim Ridge	18
51	Ure (Yorks)	10 15	July 2003	Martin Meechan	11
52	Wear (Durham)	12 02	Sept 1999	Bob Gascoigne	13
53	Welland (Lincs)	9 08	Sept 1966	Al Taylor	10
54	Wensum (Norfolk)	17 01	Oct 2003	Tim Ellis	18
55	Wey (Surrey)	14 05	Feb 2001	Steve King	16
56	Wharfe (Yorks)	13 02	Autumn 2003	James Illingworth	14
57	Windrush (Oxon)	11 09	June 1998	Danny Empson	12
58	Witham (Lincs)	9 14	Mar 2000	Colin Wilson	10
59	Wye	14 09	July 2003	Mike Easton	16
60	Yare (Norfolk)	10 01	Jan 2000	Chris Turnbull	11

*Present national record.

© Brian Dowling 05/04

this in style, recording an 11lb 1oz fish on hair-rigged meat.

Very few reports are received concerning large barbel from this river – the potential weight must be a conservative 12lb – but with the bigger Avon fish likely to move into the river to spawn, a higher weight could be possible early in the season.

Avon (Bristol)

Weight	Captor	Date
15lbs 9½oz	Stuart Morgan	Feb 1998
15lb 2oz	Martin Bowler	Nov 2002
14lb 14oz	Neville Day	Aug 1995

Rising in the Cotswolds, the river winds its way through the Wiltshire countryside entering the Severn mouth west of Bristol.

Barbel were first introduced around 1955–57 with fifty-four fish between 1–3lb released at Stokeford Bridge. Around 600 barbel were stocked at seven different points along the river during the 1960s–70s, these coming from the Enbourne, a Thames tributary.

Stuart Morgan's fish was the result of fishing an area normally ignored by anglers and fell for a John Baker paste bait, *Angler's Mail*, 11 March 1998. After moving to the area in 2000, Martin Bowler spent two winters tracking a few large fish before banking his 15lb 2oz specimen. *Angling Times*, 26 November 02. Neville Day's previous river record caused controversy despite the angling press showing a very large barbel in pristine condition.

This fish was thought to be the offspring from the hot summer of 1976 making it around 19 years old. Hot spots were recorded at Avoncliffe, Laycock, Limpley Stoke and Bradford-on-Avon.

As Morgan's fish was caught six years ago, a 16lb or 17lb fish may be possible in the next 3–4 years.

Avon (Hampshire)

Weight	Captor	Date
15lb 1oz	Jim Eggleton	Aug 2001
14lb 12oz	Dave Land	Oct 1994
14lb 12 oz	Martin Hooper	Dec 1993

The Royalty Fishery on the river is probably the most famous barbel stretch in the country, providing the national record of 14lb 6oz to the Hon. Aylmer Tyron as far back as September 1934, a record held until 1992–93.

On 28 August 2001, Jim Eggleton fishing a short after-work session, netted a huge barbel of 15lb 1oz on a paste bait. This fish took the river record from Dave Land's fish of October 1994, a gap of nearly seven years. A number of fish of over 14lb had been landed in recent years, one of the best being John O'Halloran's 14lb 8oz caught in a Downham Club match during October 2003 in torrential rain and a 50mph gale. Unfortunately this was not enough to win the match but it did break the 68-year-old official Royalty record of 14lb 6oz.

Schoolboy Ryan Gibson claimed a fish of 16lb 4oz in September 2001 while on holiday at Fordingbridge but this fish caused controversy, especially as anglers on the bank at the time believed it to be nearer 13lb. The photograph in the *Angling Times*, 2 October 2001, was difficult to judge but certainly showed a large barbel in good condition.

For his fish, Martin Hooper used a maggot feeder approach netting a 3lb roach in the same session. A red letter day!

This superb barbel weighing 13lb 11oz was the third largest recorded from the Warwickshire Avon. It was caught by Ashley Burton in February 2003.

Large barbel certainly reside in the river but it is difficult to predict when a 16lb or 17lb fish might be caught. In March, a short evening session resulted in Ringwood specialist Mark Callaway banking a 14lb 12oz barbel, joint second best from the river, being only 5oz short of the river record. Fluctuating water levels and a cold spell at the end of the season saw several 12lb and 13lb fish landed, with river guide Richard Wookey's 13lb 12oz being the best on rolling meat.

Avon (Warwickshire)

Weight	Captor	Date
15lb 3oz	Alan King	Mar 2004
14lb 10oz	Dean O'Brien	Mar 2002
13lb 11oz	Ashley Burton	Feb 2003
13lb 8oz	Kane O'Brien	Mar 2002

Rising near Naseby, the Avon runs down through Leamington and Warwick on to Stratford-upon-Avon before joining the Severn near Tewkesbury. The size of barbel caught in the last few years has dramatically increased since the mid-1990s when a 12lb 4oz fish was the best reported.

In October 1964, 117 barbel were stocked over six sites, having been removed from the river Swale in Yorkshire. Further stockings followed in 1970 (180) with an additional fifty fish from the Severn at Strensham Weir and at Warwick.

With improving water quality, the present-day barbel are showing exceptional growth rate. Ashley Burton from Hinckley is one of the most successful anglers on the river, having caught a succession of barbel over 12lb, with the best at 13lb 11oz caught on meat.

A 15lb 2oz barbel reported on 9 August 2003 by Worcester angler Dan Coley lacked any evidence. A holidaymaker took the required photograph but failed to make this available. An unconfirmed report of a 17lb fish electrofished in the late 1990s remains unsubstantiated. Early March 2004 saw the river record of 14lb 10oz broken by a huge barbel at 15lb 3oz from the Manor Farm Leisure Caravan Park by Hereford angler Alan King. The fish was weighed and witnessed by Manor Farm boss David Byrd, and is the first authenticated 15lb fish from the up and coming river. Successful bait was the popular halibut pellet.

Blackwater (Berkshire)

Weight	Captor	Date
11lb 4oz	Bob Vince	Aug 1999

A tributary of the river Loddon, the Blackwater can be susceptible to flooding. A handful of specialists fish the river for barbel, but catches are generally shrouded in secrecy, most fish being caught at night in high water conditions. The 11lb fish came from the Cove AS stretch, but photographs were not published, although the fish was witnessed.

However, two other barbel, along with a sizeable mirror carp, were included in an *Angler's Mail* feature page. Rumours of larger fish being caught remain unconfirmed.

Cherwell (Oxon)

Weight	Captor	Date
13lb	Michael Coleman	Oct 2002
12lb 14oz	Geoff Osman	Mar 2003

This is a small Thames tributary running into the main river at Oxford. Local anglers report little of what they catch, with probably only a small number of large barbel resident in the river. This may lead to recaptures at different weights. Brackley angler Michael Coleman used a pellet covered in paste to tempt his river record

Michael Harvey with a 12-pounder caught in the River Cherwell in March 2000.

when the river was 2ft above normal, on a Gerrards Cross stretch.

The 12lb 14oz fish fell to Geoff Osman in the last few days of the 2002–03 season and is thought to be the same fish as Coleman's. Although Tony Miles and Simon Lush held the river record back in 1989 after much pioneering work, it was thought that Oxford angler Andy Webber held the record at 12lb 12oz in 1993, but the measurement of 27½in × 17¼in didn't equate to such a weight, with specialist anglers questioning the fish, stating that it was actually 10lb 12oz!

Colne (Middlesex)

Weight	Captor	Date
15lb 5oz	Paul Jebb	Jan 2002
13lb 7oz	Chris Crook	Nov 2003

The old NRA carried out stockings of small barbel into the river in 1993, 1995,

1996, and the Gerrards Cross AC stocked large numbers of fish in the 1–3lb class in 1996 at Rickmansworth.

Barbel are few and far between on the river but average around 8lb which makes predicting a potential weight for future fish extremely difficult. The most productive stretches are at West Drayton, Denham and Uxbridge, plus the river close to Heathrow Airport, it having produced a 12lb fish a few years ago, but plans have been made to add another runway that could result in the course of the river being changed at this point.

Paul Jebb of West Hendon made a hasty decision to go barbel fishing since conditions felt right, and at 8pm on 29 January 2002 his hunch paid off. He surprised the specimen world with a huge fish of 15lb 5oz caught using a Guy Robb 12ft barbel rod, the bait being Mainline boilie.

Chris Crook of Staines netted a 13lb 7oz fish on casters in November 2003. Several

Paul Jebb with a 15lb 15oz short, fat, carp-like barbel taken from the Colne on 29 January 2002. This fish is the Colne record.

fish over 12lb have been caught in the last few years, but some of these may well be recaptures. It was rumoured that a 14lb 3oz barbel was caught in early January 2004 and that one or two large barbel (over 16lb) had been electrofished in 2003 – both with no photographic evidence.

Dane (Cheshire)

Weight	Captor	Date
14lb 4oz	Phil Booth	Aug 1994

This is a small river, full of character, that flows from the Peak District through Cheshire and out into the sea in Liverpool Bay. Barbel were first introduced in 1970 from the river Severn, with further stockings following in 1984 and 1993.

A 14lb 4oz barbel caught by Phil Booth in August 1994 lacks evidence, although some local anglers consider the capture to be a genuine one. Shunning publicity and moving to Canada has hindered obtaining photographic evidence.

In February 2002 the Bay Malton Angling Club produced a newsletter claiming that a 15lb barbel had been caught and witnessed, but no evidence was ever produced. A 15lb 6oz barbel attributed to Paul Forester also remains a mystery. With Booth's fish being caught ten years ago, indications are that there are only a handful of very large, old barbel in the river and a 10lb fish is still an excellent capture.

Derwent (Derbyshire)

Weight	Captor	Date
12lb 11oz	Jamie Alexander	Nov 2003
10lb 6oz	Clive Ruddy	Jan 2002

Known as a notoriously difficult river, the Derwent has often provided matchmen with smashed-up tackle – all put down to large barbel. With various rumours circulating regarding the capture of a 12lb barbel, it was no surprise to hear of Jamie Alexander's 12lb 11oz fish from a stretch at Borrowash. He added other fish including a specimen of 10lb 2oz all on pellet/paste baits. *Anglers Mail*, 6 December 2003 report, but due to poor quality the photograph was never published. Thomas Petch of the *Mail* stated that the fish looked totally genuine at its claimed weight.

Clive Ruddy using a feeder approach topped a four fish catch with a 10lb 6oz specimen.

Derwent (Yorkshire)

Weight	Captor	Date
12lb 6oz	Jon Wolfe	Sept 1989
12lb 2oz	Bob Goodison	June 1999

The Derwent rises on Fylingdales Moor some 850ft above sea level and is around 77 miles long, entering the Ouse at Barmby on Marsh. The NRA introduced 14,000 chub and barbel into the river in 1993 but large barbel have always been scarce.

Fifteen years have elapsed since Jon Wolfe's fish that is generally accepted as the river record, despite several large fish being claimed. A barbel of 12lb 8oz mentioned in the angling press in the early 1990s failed to materialize with evidence of capture, although it is known that Yorkshire specialist Dave Mason had one over 12lb!

If the handful of old fish have now died off it would be almost impossible to predict a future weight potential for the river, especially as the biggest floods in living memory occurred in the winter of 1998–99 washing any remaining fry away.

The ever-increasing demands of abstraction by the water authorities is also cause for concern. Stretches at Kirkham Abbey and Kexby Bridge may offer the best chance of a specimen.

Don (Yorkshire)

Weight	Captor	Date
8lb 4oz	Christian Lawrence	Sept 2002

Once called the most polluted river in Britain, it is now vastly improved.

The 8lb barbel caught by Christian Lawrence is certainly not the largest fish in the river, as locals know of several fish caught around 10lb. Barbel are on the increase, with Sprotborough Weir near Doncaster being a favourite hot spot!

Dove (Staffordshire)

Weight	Captor	Date
13lb 8oz	Mike Hamilton	Oct 2001
13lb 4oz	John Arkwright	Sept 2000
13lb 3oz	Steve Stayner	Mar 1999

Although a near 10lb barbel was caught back in the 1950s this Trent tributary has only taken off in the last 5–7 years as a productive barbel river. It was previously known as a salmon spawning ground, a recent sighting (2001) being made by an EA Fisheries officer, but prior to this the last time a salmon was spotted on the river was back in the 1930s.

Mike Hamilton's fish was caught on a Prince Albert stretch on 4 October 2001 using a Seer Rod and John Baker paste as bait. The club's publicity ban had stopped a photograph being made available, but the capture is a genuine one and witnesses are available.

However, John Arkwright's monster was featured on the front cover of the *Prince Albert Newsletter*, issue 45, dated February 2001. Due to work commitments John was living in a caravan on the banks of the river, the fish accepting a lobworm in floodwater conditions. Steve Stayner's fish was the same as the previous river record at 12lb 9oz in Oct 1998. Rumours abound about three 14lb fish and it may not be too long before a genuine fish of this weight turns up.

A fish of 13lb 3oz was landed by Geoff Dace, a Barbel Catchers Club member from a known big barbel swim in Staffordshire and was featured in a photograph published in the BCC book, *Barbel Rivers and Captures*, published by Crowood in April 2004.

Ember (Surrey)

Weight	Captor	Date
9lb 4oz	Seb Pizzuto	Aug 2001
9lb 1oz	Lou Hart	Aug 1994

This is a narrow Thames tributary that runs into the main river via the River Mole at Hampton Court. Barbel are rarely reported from this tiny river. In a revised listing, Seb Pizzuto's barbel, caught on meat, heads the list. The photo was published in the *Angler's Mail* on 8 September 2001. Due to lack of photographic evidence a 9lb 4oz fish reported by Keith Williams in August 1994 has been dropped.

Frome (Somerset)

Weight	Captor	Date
10lb 15oz	Andy Cowley	Aug 1995

A small tributary of the Bristol Avon with its own head of barbel, Andy Cowley's fish was captured from a stretch several miles from the source with the Avon and may have had its origins in a small stocking made during the late 1980s and not a traveller from the Avon as first thought. It measured 29½in × 16½in with a photograph in the *Coarse Angling Today* magazine.

A fish claimed at 12lb 6oz by 11-year-old Michael Ashwin while fishing with his father at Fairleigh Hungerford in September 1994 was hotly disputed, and the photograph in the *Angler's Mail*, October 1994 did nothing to substantiate the claim.

A genuine 12lb fish could be a possibility but very few specimens are ever reported.

Holybrook (Kennet Tributary)

Weight	Captor	Date
13lb 4oz	Trevor King	Oct 2003
10lb 10oz	John Sheldon	Dec 1998

A tiny tributary of the river Kennet in Berkshire, it runs for 4 miles leaving the main river at Theale rejoining it in the centre of Reading. Although Reading District Angling Association control some stretches, most remain in private hands.

In the 1990s a 13lb barbel was reported to the *Angler's Mail* but with no supporting evidence. Trevor King mentioned that a 14lb fish had been rumoured, but no evidence was forthcoming (2002–03). In the Barbel Catchers Club book, *Barbel Rivers and Captures* (April 2004), Trevor King is shown holding the river record fish at 13lb 4oz which was caught on pellet.

Ivel (Bedfordshire)

Weight	Captor	Date
13lb 2oz	Keith Smith	Mar 2004
13lb	Mark Elt	Sept 2003
12lb 11oz	Alan Rumble	Oct 2002
12lb 6oz	Mark Worbey	Aug 2003

This tiny river is a tributary of the Great Ouse, running from Tempsford, north of Bedford, down to Letchworth Blunham and Biggleswade. Over 7,000 small barbel were stocked during 1994–95 with a 10lb 4oz fish reported from Langford Mill around February/March 1995.

A decision to walk the banks before fishing paid off for Huntingdon angler Mark Elt who spotted some large barbel under trees in a low clear river. After pre-baiting he returned in mid-afternoon latching onto the fish at 4pm. *Angling Times* photo, 16 September 2003 showed a barbel in pristine condition.

Local Biggleswade landscape gardener Keith Smith claimed a late-season river record with a stunning 13lb 2oz fish, caught on 6lb line falling for trotted maggot. *Angler's Mail* photograph, 27 March 04.

Hitchen angler Alan Rumble used prawns on the hook after spotting small crayfish – for a specimen of 12lb 11oz. *Angling Times*, 29 October 2002. Bedford design engineer Mark Worbey tempted his specimen with a boilie, having witnessed Alan Rumble's fish the previous October.

If these fish pack on weight a recapture is likely at around 15lb in a season or two.

Kennet (Berkshire)

Weight	Captor	Date
16lb 10oz	Edward Barder	Feb 2002
16lb 8oz	Jeff Coultas	Jan 2004
16lb 4oz	Paul Smythe	Oct 2003
16lb 3oz	Richard Wallis	Oct 2003

A Thames tributary, the Kennet has provided stocks of small barbel to many of the country's rivers, including the river Severn (509 fish in 1956), Dorset Stour (1,896)

Edward Barder with his beautiful Kennet record barbel weighing 16lb 10oz that he caught in February 2002.

Paul Smythe holds his 16lb 4oz barbel that he caught in the Kennet in October 2003.

Keith Matthews holds the seventh joint Kennet record with this fine fish weighing 15lb 13oz that he caught in February 2003.

and the Hampshire Avon in the 1960s, along with the Bristol Avon.

Edward Barder of rod building fame lives close to the river and, at present, holds the river record with a fish caught on 13 February 2002 with a water temperature at just 47°F. It measured 30½in × 20½in and was thought to be around 30 years old. A number of large specimens over 15lb have been landed in the last 2–3 seasons by several anglers, leading to the conclusion that many of these are recaptures.

Paul Smythe's fish came from a weirpool and fell to a C.C. Moores boilie. It took a Ray Walton Harrison 1.6 River Roller rod to land the specimen. Former matchman Richard Wallis caught his 16lb 3oz fish plus another of 12lb 1oz on frozen ready-made boilies from an undisclosed stretch. Hungerford specialist Jeff Coultas banked a brace of barbel for 26lb 10oz on ledgered lobworm from a high river in Jan 2004. With four barbel in just two hours his catch included a fish of 10lb 2oz and a monster of 16lb 8oz this being just 2oz short of Edward Barder's February 2002 record.

Rumours of an 18lb 2oz barbel remain unsubstantiated, although the river must be very close to producing its first 18lb fish.

Lea

Weight	Captor	Date
15lb ½oz	Jason Shaw	March 2002
14lb 14oz	Terry Ettridge	Feb 2004
14lb 8oz	Kevin Newton	Jan 2004
14lb 8oz	Terry Ettridge	March 2002
14lb 5oz	Mark Wilson	Feb 2004

The river rises north of Dunstable winding its way down through Hertfordshire and North London before joining the Thames near Greenwich. It was stocked many years ago with barbel by the old Thames Water authority and illegally by anglers around Hertford. In the early 1990s, the river's fish population suffered badly from diseases as

This is the third largest barbel from the river Lea. It was caught at Fishers Green by Kevin Newton in January 2004 and weighed 14lb 8oz.

a result of increasing effluent going into the river particularly in low-water conditions. Thankfully, since water privatization in 1989 huge amounts of money have been invested in sewage treatment schemes, and today the river is producing healthy fish.

Barbel were conspicuous by their absence as temperatures dropped in the last few days of the season (2003–04). However, Enfield angler, Raymond Cann managed a 14lb 4oz one from Fishers Green on pellet.

Jason Shaw's fish caused controversy as the published photograph did little to suggest that it was a 15lb barbel. However, it was witnessed by several anglers and stands today as the only 15lb fish recorded.

Terry Ettridge, a carpenter from Tower Hamlets, London, came within a couple of ounces of the river record on 14 February 2004, with a huge barbel of 14lb 14oz. The fish was tempted on bacon grill, Terry's normal bait which also lured a fish of 14lb 8oz in March 2002.

Kevin Newton used a Harrison 12ft × 1½ TC rod and a boilie to bank a specimen of 14lb 8oz in January 2004, at Fishers Green. *Angling Times* photo, 24 February 2004.

Another late-season entry was Ilford angler Mark Wilson's excellent fish at 14lb 5oz during a short 3-hour session into darkness on 14 February, the same day that Terry Ettridge banked his 14lb 14oz giant.

As probably only a handful of fish in the river have the potential to beat the 16lb barrier, it is likely that when the record is finally broken, it will be a known fish that is recorded.

Leam (Warwickshire)

Weight	Captor	Date
11lb 9oz	Trevor Kennedy	March 2000

A tiny tributary of the Warwickshire Avon,

this river was well known for its chub catches back in the 1960s–70s, but has little track record for barbel. Trevor Kennedy's fish came as a total surprise, especially as his previous best was one fish of 5lb. Fishing a swim at Offchurch the fish fell for ledgered meat.

Loddon (Berkshire)

Weight	Captor	Date
15lb 15oz	Paul West	Oct 2002
14lb 8oz	Phil Perrin	Nov 2002

This is a small tributary of the Thames that joins the main river east of Reading. Although only a small stream in places it has a growing reputation for large barbel.

The river record might have been broken in the last week of the 2002–03 season when North London angler Nick Coulhurst latched onto a 16lb 1oz barbel. The pictures submitted to the angling press were too blurred with the angler's hands covering the fish, with the result that it was never published.

Paul West only started fishing for barbel in June 2001, having moved over from fly fishing. He fished a short after-work session casting a paste bait which was accepted by the huge fish within a minute of touching bottom. After a spirited fight the fish was witnessed by several club officials from an undisclosed stretch. It was the Caversham Anglers thirteen barbel – lucky for some!

Soldier Phil Perrin caught his 14lb 8oz fish from a Fareham AS Club stretch after a run of five blanks, the fish falling for curry-flavoured spam.

A 17lb fish could be on the cards in the next two seasons.

A photograph of a barbel of 15lb 14oz as shown in the BCC book, *Barbel Rivers and Captures*, published by Crowood Press, but it was unclear as to the captor's name, especially as the fish did not feature in the BCC Top 50 Fish List.

Lugg (Herefordshire)

Weight	Captor	Date
10lb 8oz	Darren Godsall	July 1999

A Wye tributary, this small river runs through Lugwardine near Hereford, down to Mordiford and Hampton Bishop where it joins the Wye. It is a scenic river that produces specimen barbel most seasons.

Darren Godsall, a Hereford angler, used feeder tactics to beat his barbel reported with a photo in the *Angling Times*, dated 21 July 1999. A 10lb 12oz fish, caught in 1994 by Mike Burdon, a Barbel Catchers Club member, was never reported to the press.

Mease (Staffordshire)

Weight	Captor	Date
13lb	Phil Hart	Nov 1996

This is a tiny river running through Staffordshire that comes into its own in the winter months, with both chub and barbel. The controlling club on the stretch where Phil Hart caught his fish enforced a publicity ban but, despite this, *Angling Times* published a photograph on 16 November 1996. Barbel stocks appear to be very low.

Medway (Kent)

Weight	Captor	Date
16lb 2oz	Pete Woodhouse	Jun 1994*
16lb 1oz	Chris Spaulding	Sept 2003
15lb 15oz	Kevin Colston Iles	Mar 1995
15lb 13oz	Chris Spaulding	Sept 2003
15lb 11oz	Andy Harman	Sept 1993*
15lb 7oz	Bob Morris	Jan 1993*

*Previous national record holders.

Running through the lovely countryside of East Sussex and Kent, the river in places resembles a small stream. Fifty small barbel were stocked by the old Kent River Authority in 1959 but it was not until the late 1980s that large barbel began to turn up. These were thought to be survivors of the original stocking.

In the mid-1990s it produced no fewer than six national barbel records including Peter Woodhouse's current river record caught on the opening day in June 1994. It was thought that most, if not all of these fish, consisted of just one barbel nicknamed 'Bertie' by the Fleet Street press (it appeared in a national daily) but was actually a female fish. For many years the reports of huge barbel dried up but in September 2003, local Tunbridge angler Chris Spaulding put in a concentrated effort on the river, resulting in fish of 16lb 1oz, 15lb 13oz, 14lb 7oz and 12lb 4oz providing proof that the river is coming back to its best.

All this could indicate that a 17lb barbel may be a possibility at the back end of a season. Stories abound concerning a 17lb barbel caught twice(!) and one of 19lb but both lack evidence. The river now appears to hold barbel of all sizes with the Fordcombe and Ashurst stretches generally offering the best chance of a monster.

Mole (Surrey)

Weight	Captor	Date
13lb 5oz	Paul Starkey	Jan 2003
13lb 4oz	Terry Smith	Feb 2002
12lb 14oz	Luke Anderson	Oct 2003

Another small tributary, this river has seen many changes, including being re-routed around Gatwick Airport. The first change occurred in 1956 due to culvert work under the runway, then in the 1980s prior to work commencing on the North

Terminal. In 1999, further changes took place due to expansion. The river meanders across Surrey through the North Downs, joining the Thames below Moseley Weir near Hampton Court.

Paul Starkey, a BCC member, caught his fish in January 2003 beating Terry Smith's record by just 1oz. This appeared to be the same fish. Terry's fish fell for curried frankfurter, beating his previous best of just 6lb 7oz. The fish was recognized as one caught in 2000 at 10lb 4oz having an easily recognizable split tail fin.

Luke Anderson took three years to catch his first barbel in 2003, topping his captures with a pristine 12lb 14oz on meat. A 12lb fish caught by David Whitehead was incorrectly stated as the river record in August 2002 by the *Angling Times*. A 14lb 9oz barbel claimed by Dave Steer during October 2002 remains a mystery despite a phone call to the *Angler's Mail* offices. Although claiming the fish, no evidence of details of the match were provided.

More controversy was caused when a photograph appeared in the *Angler's Mail*, 28 February 2004 showing a barbel claimed to be 17lb caught by Marc Cousins. A photograph displayed in the Surbiton Angling Centre caused local anglers to question both the weight and exact location where the fish was caught. One previous record holder stated that Mole fish were generally long and slim but with this fish being very short and stocky it appeared to be more 'Ouse'-like in appearance.

Nene (Northants)

Weight	Captor	Date
12lb	Dave Williams	June 1969

Although known as a big carp water around Peterborough in the 1950s–60s, the river has only rarely produced barbel of note, despite a stocking organized by the *Angling Times* in the late 1950s.

In 1993–94 some 14,000 small barbel were introduced and, in the last couple of years, reports have filtered through of double-figure fish being caught.

The 12lb fish caught by sixth-former David Williams in 1969 received much publicity in the *Angling Times*, being witnessed by Peter Tombleson, secretary of the Record Fish Committee.

As no photographic evidence has been provided, Brian Simister's 12lb 8oz barbel caught in July 2000 has been put on hold, in the hope that a photograph will become available.

Local anglers are keeping catches to themselves but carp legend Duncan Kay has probably caught the best fish so far, with a weight of 13lb. Although a photograph has been seen, it has been withheld, the angler wishing to shun all publicity.

Nidd (Yorkshire)

Weight	Captor	Date
11lb 4oz	Phil Johnson	Oct 1993

This is a delightful little river that runs through the Yorkshire Dales joining the Ouse, 10 miles above York at Moor Monkton.

Although considered for many years as the river record, Ken Smith's 12lb 11oz 1977 barbel had doubts surrounding its capture. The angler phoned the late Alan Howe who, at the time, was angling correspondent for the *Yorkshire Evening Post*. Alan then reported the capture in good faith, but it was later revealed that no photographs had been taken, and that there were no witnesses. A 12lb 8oz fish thought to have been caught in 1963 was never substantiated.

A genuine capture was Phil Johnson's fish caught in a match run by the Thorner

Steve Curtin with his best Great Ouse barbel for the 2003–04 season. This magnificent fish known as 'Stumpy' weighed 18lb 6oz and was caught on 10 January 2004.

Mexborough AC on the river at Hammerton. Jon Wolfe had previously stalked this fish hooking it near some snags but eventually losing it. Phil's second cast produced the fish that took twenty minutes to land and was witnessed by club officials. Seven pounds is still a big barbel for the river but larger fish regularly migrate up from the Ouse to spawn below Kirk Hammerton weir in the early part of the season. Other hotspots are Tockwith and around the Skipbridge area.

Ouse, Great

Weight	Captor	Date
19lb 6½oz	Steve Curtin	Oct 2001
19lb 2oz	Stuart Court	Sept 2003
19lb 2oz	Tony Miles	Feb 2002
19lb	Tony Gibson	Jan 2001

For a more detailed listing of Great Ouse barbel refer to the UK listing. The river is some 150 miles long rising from a limestone spring above Brackley, Northants, and flowing into the sea at King's Lynn in Norfolk. A great deal of activity is centred around the area 'above' Bedford, including stretches at Adams Mill and Kickles Farm.

The river at present appears to be the only one in the country likely to yield a 20lb barbel. Many fish over 15lb are now caught each season, with fish having 'names' leading to many recaptures taking place.

Stockings occurred in the 1950s, again in 1969 and throughout the 1990s, when over 20,000 fish were introduced at different points along the river. Steve Curtin's record barbel at 19lb 6½oz caught in Oct 2001, remains the country's best, despite concentrated efforts by some of the top barbel experts at the 'back end' of each season. The fish known as the 'Pope' at present evades capture, since Tony Gibson recorded it in January 2001, at 19lbs. This fish has been spotted in the company of other barbel and appears to have put on considerable weight, leading to much speculation.

Unfortunately, Steve Curtin's fish known as 'Red Belly' was found dead on the banks of Adams Mill back in September 2002 when it recorded 19lb 8oz, although an amount of water had been absorbed. The fish was thought to be between 20–25 years old having died of old age.

Trevor King, a well-known taxidermist is in the process of setting up the fish with its final destination likely to be the London Natural History Museum. On setting up the fish it was concluded that it was probably a hermaphrodite – carrying both male and female sexual organs, effectively giving it an entirely different biological makeup from normal barbel. This inbalance could cause the fish to put more effort into feeding and growth rather than spawning.

Should other fish in the river contain similar makeup then this might go some way to explaining why the Ouse produces the size of fish that is far above those of other rivers in the country. Any change of a sexual nature in fish is likely to be caused by substances in the water consisting of thousands of chemicals, with the balance of such chemicals being crucial.

Another fish likely to push the current best is 'The Traveller' caught by both Stuart Court in September 2003 from an 'impossible' swim and Tony Miles at the same weight of 19lb 2oz. This fish has a

distinctive cut out of its tail and has also been caught by Adrian Busby at 18lb 12oz (October 2003), Vince Rogers (November 2003) at 18lb 11oz and Guy Robb (January 2003) at 18lb 10oz.

After a mixture of hard frosts and cold rain the last few weeks of the season, (2003–04) saw only a handful of very big barbel landed. The last weekend in March 2004 failed to see water temperatures rise to more than 44°F, having remained around 41°F for long spells.

Steve Curtin caught the same fish ('Stumpy') twice in January/February 2004 at 18lb 6oz and 18lb 5oz from the same swim, landing both on his new Edward Barder split-cane rod. Warren Gaunt returned a 17lb 1oz fish in February 2004 from the Newport Pagnell stretch, making him the first person to achieve a unique angling treble, having banked 17lb plus zander, bream and barbel. He used a 1½lb TC Harrison rod and a DT boilie.

In the same month, river regular Grahame King achieved his half century of double-figure barbel with a 16lb fish, followed just hours later with a 14lb 6oz

UK Top Barbel – Great Ouse at 1 December 2004

Weight		Captor	Date	Fish known
lb	oz		Month/Year	as
20	06	Tony Gibson	Oct 2004	'The Traveller'
20	04	David Swindley	Oct 2004	'The Traveller'
19	06½	Steve Curtin	Oct 2001	'Red Belly'
19	02	Stuart Court	Sept 2003	'The Traveller'
19	02	Tony Miles	Feb 2002	'The Traveller'
19	00	Tony Gibson	Jan 2001	'The Pope'
18	13½	Ray Walton	Jan 2002	'Red Belly'
18	13	Vince Rogers	Feb 2002	'Red Belly'
18	12	Adrian Busby	Oct 2003	'The Traveller'
18	12	Dave Green	Nov 2001	'Red Belly'
18	11	Vince Rogers	Nov 2003	'The Traveller'
18	10	Guy Robb	Jan 2003	'The Traveller'
18	09	Tony Miles	Dec 2002	'Stumpy'
18	06	Steve Curtin	Jan 2004	'Stumpy'

Kevin Colston-Iles with his 11lb 8½oz Sussex Ouse record fish that he caught in October 2002.

barbel making a huge brace of 30lb 6oz. In a previous session, he had landed a 15lb 8oz fish on John Baker boilie. On the last Friday of the season (12 March) Ray Walton extracted a 15lb 7oz fish to complete a disappointing end to a difficult season. All eyes will be on the river's barbel population come June 2004.

Ouse (Sussex)

Weight	Captor	Date
11lb 8½oz	K. Colston-Iles	Oct 2000
10lb 10oz	Danny Rumble	July 1998

The first recorded introduction of barbel involved eighty fish between 2lb and 8lb in 1974 from the river Severn. Exact details are not known as some of these fish were also placed into the Arun and Adur rivers in the county.

Five hundred fish to 6in reared at Calverton Fish Farm at Nottingham went into the river at Barcombe in early 1993 at the request of the Ouse Preservation AS and the Sussex Piscatorials. They reported that a few barbel introduced during 1992 had survived and spawned.

A further 1,000 fish were stocked in 1999. In the spring of 2003, a chemical spill from a company producing strawberry

colouring resulted in many species of coarse fish being washed away in the tidal parts of the river. There was no mention of barbel being affected.

Barbel specialist Kevin Colston-Iles moved away from his favourite Medway to capture the heaviest witnessed fish record.

Danny Rumble's fish featured on an *Angler's Mail* feature page. Lindfield and higher up on the weir pools around Haywards Heath could produce the river's first 12lb fish.

Ouse (Yorkshire)

Weight	Captor	Date
10lb 10oz	John McNulty	Sept 1998
10lb 8oz	Mr Thornton	1953
10lb 4oz	M. Baron	1944
10lb 2oz	RAF Sgt Crawley	1950s

Wide (in places over 33yd), deep (well over 20ft) and at times featureless, the river generally takes second place to most other Yorkshire rivers for barbel, especially as mild spells in the autumn/winter months are often accompanied by serious flooding.

Although reported, Mr Rogers' 12lb 12oz fish in July 1935 and Mr G. Dean's fish at 12lb½oz in 1958 both lacked firm evidence and nowadays any Ouse fish over 9lb is considered a huge specimen. A genuine, witnessed capture was that of John McNulty, a Barbel Catchers Club member, in September 1998 with a barbel of 10lb 10oz. Present-day reports from the river generally refer to fish in the 6–8lb class. A 10lb 12oz barbel caught by S. 'Ginger' Tittener in 1955 from Linton was photographed but this was not made available. A photograph of M. Baron's 10lb 4oz barbel was featured in the February 2003 edition of the *Coarse Angling Today* magazine. Mr Crawley's 10lb 2oz fish was witnessed by John Nixon of Redmire carp fame. However, the areas below Linton Lock, such as Newton and Beningborough, are the areas likely to produce better quality fish. There are known larger fish in the river, but captures over the present record are difficult to substantiate.

Potts Stream (Oxford)

Weight	Captor	Date
13lb 8oz	John Ginifer	Oct 1968
12lb 8oz	Gwynn Williams	1963
11lb 4oz	Fred J. Taylor	1959

Potts Stream, a tiny side stream off the Thames in Oxford, produced some large barbel to over 13lb back in the 1960s. Several large barbel were attributed to the river Thames in those days when they had, in fact, been caught from Potts.

The stream silted up many years ago, probably due to the increase in motorized boat traffic on the main river and abstraction, combined with the effect of agricultural pollution. John Ginifer, a schoolmaster from Hemingford Grey, recorded the stream's best barbel at 13lb 8oz. He also claimed to have spotted barbel estimated at around 20lb, when peering over the side of his canoe.

Ribble (Lancashire)

Weight	Captor	Date
14lb 7oz	Mark Halstead	Mar 2002
14lb 5oz	Neil McIver	Feb 2002
14lb 4oz	Paul Bennett	Nov 2003

Barbel in the river were stocked from the Swale in the 1960s and then from the river Severn in the 1970s, when illegal stockings were shipped up the M6. In October 1993, 2000 dye-marked barbel were introduced on the Tickled Trout hotel stretch near Preston. As a result of these stockings the river is ever-improving regarding barbel catches, with the back end of the season 2001–02 being particularly productive.

The river returned to form at the end of the season, with local expert Paul Bennett banking barbel of 13lb 15½oz and 12lb 10oz, the larger fish being the fourth over 13lb this season. Both fish were beaten on 12lb mainline and homemade boilies wrapped in paste.

Mark Halstead's fish was the reward for a one-man crusade in order to prove the river's barbel potential. The record breaker measured 32in × 18¾in and fell to a paste bait.

Fishing the upper reaches, Preston angler Neil McIver used corn to fool his specimen which was caught during torrential rain.

Paul Bennett's barbel fell to home-made boilies over hemp and pellets and was included in a catch of five doubles over two days. Harrison 'Chimera' rods and 5000 GTE reels completed the tackle picture.

A 14lb 6oz barbel credited to Phil Douglas is considered genuine with a photograph residing in Ted Carter's tackle shop in Preston.

Another barbel of 14lb 4oz reported in November 2003 claimed by Roger Nowell failed to have a picture published due to poor quality.

This wonderful 15lb 7oz barbel was caught by Steve Whyborn in February 2002.

In December 1998, a 16lb (exactly!) fish was claimed by Jim Hilton, but the only photograph published showed the fish on a sack, and this failed to convince specialist anglers in the area and was not considered a record.

Late-season activity (2003–4) saw river regular Mark Halstead put in a concentrated effort after the first 15lb barbel from the river. February 2004 saw him bank a 14lb 1oz fish together with ones of 11lb 14oz, 11lb 3oz and 10lb 14oz in a nine-fish haul, all this after losing a large barbel in a snag. Successful bait was a home-made paste.

In the last few days of the season, he landed a 14lb 4oz fish ending a successful campaign despite poor weather conditions.

On an ever improving river, top-spots are at Balderstone, Hayhurst and Salmersbury.

Rother (Sussex)

Weight	Captor	Date
12lb 12oz	Pete Foster	Jan 2004

This beautiful tiny river flows into the muddy waters of the Arun below Pulborough. In the 1980s barbel were stocked at Shopham Bridge and Littleworth. The fish subsequently caught were between 6lb and 8lb but were few in number.

Peter Foster's 10lb 3oz caught at Coultershaw Bridge, is thought to be the first properly authenticated 'double' to come from the river. The angling press held back the photograph as the quality was poor, but they were happy to accept the weight of the fish as stated.

Peter followed this fish with a river record in January 2004 banking a 12lb 12oz specimen from the same area on 14mm Halibut pellet. A fish of 11lb 4oz was rumoured but no photographs were available. It is thought that the river could produce its first 13lb at the back end of a season.

St Patrick's Stream (Berkshire)

Weight	Captor	Date
15lb 8oz	Keith Evans	Oct 2001
15lb 7oz	Steve Whyborn	Feb 2002
15lb ½oz	Dave Currell	Dec 2000

This is a lovely little Berkshire backwater tributary of the river Thames. Keith Evans, a BCC member, caught his river record fish at night on 27 October 2001, thought to be the same fish as the 15lb 7oz one caught in February 2002. Steve Whyborn's fish fell to rolling meat on a Harrison Rod combined with a Ray Walton Rolling Pin Reel. The fish measured 31in. A 12lb 4oz was caught in the same session for a brace total of 27lb 11oz.

Dave Currell's fish was caught in driving rain and gales during December 2000 as the light faded.

As the river links the Thames at Sonning and the Loddon at Wargrave, it is possible that large barbel enter the stream in the early part of the season, or during winter floods. Certainly a 16lb fish is on the cards, although the small stream gets extremely crowded in the summer months.

Severn

Weight	Captor	Date
16lb 3oz	Howard Maddocks	Nov 1997
15lb 15oz	David Jenkins	Feb 1998
15lb 8oz	Charles Philbin	Oct 1993
15lb 7oz	John Costello	Oct 1998

The mighty Severn – 220 miles of river flowing out of the Welsh mountains – ends its journey in the Bristol Channel.

A barbel explosion took place in the 1970s–80s, resulting in stretches being dominated by small barbel (mainly up to 5lb). The barbel picture is different today, with mainly larger fish being spread throughout the river system, most of the specimen fish being located between Worcester and Tewkesbury.

Howard Maddock's UK record barbel, caught in November 1997, came from near Upton and was caught from a river running 14ft up on normal.

Solihull angler David Jenkins fishing at the top end of Beauchamp Court below Worcester landed the second largest barbel from the river on a Teme Tamer rod and spicy meat bait. The fish came as the light faded and was witnessed by a fellow Barbel Society member.

Charles Philbin, a disabled angler, float fishing for roach with just 2lb main line, surprised the specimen world with what must rate as an amazing angling

Howard Maddocks, accompanied by some well-known faces, displays his 16lb 3oz Severn River record barbel in November 1997.

Chris Ponsford with his splendid 15lb 5oz barbel (2001).

achievement – the fish coming from Severn Stoke.

John Costello's giant at 15lb 7oz was caught at 10.15pm on 6 October 1998 on spicy meat and measured 31¾in × 18in. Several other fish over 15lb have been caught from the river since 1997, but with Maddocks' fish being caught nearly seven years ago, it is difficult to estimate a possible potential figure for barbel in the next two to three years.

However, 17lb and 18lb barbel must be present in such a volume of water.

Soar (Leicestershire)

Weight	Captor	Date
10lb 10oz	Tony Swann	Feb 2002
10lb 1oz	John Webb	Feb 2003
10lb	Andy Lister	Nov 2002

This river alternates between a canal fishery and the 'old' river course that runs into the Trent near Long Eaton. In some places the high banks and excessive vegetation make access difficult, and after years of being a favoured match venue

the river is becoming a specialist venue, with barbel, chub and some large carp on offer. Barbel are becoming the sought-after species.

Tony Swann's fish is certainly not the largest barbel in the river as an 11lb 4oz was caught in a match in July 2003. So far no other details are available.

Local anglers know of a 12lb barbel caught some two years ago but this fish also lacks evidence. The average barbel is around 4–5lbs but a genuine 12-pounder is possible.

Sow (Staffordshire)

Weight	Captor	Date
10lb ½oz	Stewart Bloor	Sept 2002

Sedgeley angler Stewart Bloor took a fish of 10lb on a boilie fished at night.

Barbel around 9lb have been caught since 1992 from this small upper Trent tributary that flows through the town of Stafford. The natural river survives south of the town, the Izaak Walton Club controlling stretches at Brancote and Milford.

Stour (Dorset)

Weight	Captor	Date
16lb 2oz	Graham Sale	Feb 2003
15lb 12oz	Tony Snow	Feb 2003
15lb 10oz	Terry Lampard	Feb 2000
15lb 8oz	Jim Clarke	Mar 2003

Over the years, the river has become one of the most popular and prolific fisheries in the country for specimen chub and barbel. The famous Throop fishery covers some 5 miles and is a noted area for large barbel. It has been estimated that between 120 and 150 specimen barbel are landed each year. Top spots are at Longham, Muscliff and West Parley. February 2003 proved to be a good month for Southampton biochemist, Graham Sale, who took a 16lb 2oz fish from the Throop fishery, beating Terry Lampard's record fish of 15lb 10oz. It is thought to be the same as Ian Head's 15lb 5oz fish (December 2002) and that caught by Martin Bowler at 14lb 12oz (November 2002). The fish measured 30in × 20in girth. Longham Bridge was the venue for the capture of a 15lb 12oz barbel for Poole angler Tony Snow. The successful method was Method feeder. Dairy farm manager Dave Charles achieved a brace of barbel in March 2003 weighing 15lb 1oz and 14lb 2oz, making this the best brace away from the Great Ouse.

Jim Clarke achieved a personal best barbel with a fish of 15lb 8oz having previously netted a specimen of 12lb 10oz twenty-four hours earlier. Paste baits were the most successful. One of the most successful barbel anglers on the river over many seasons has been Blanford-based Terry Lampard. He followed a 14lb 6oz fish in December 2003 with a 14lb 3oz barbel in early March 2004, on Trigga paste.

Other notable fish include Bournemouth specialist Gary Steven's one at 15lb 4oz in November 2003 on a single Trigga

boilie, and Tim Norman's 15lb 3oz fish taken in gin-clear water during September 2003, again on Trigga bait. A genuine 17lb barbel must be on the cards soon, but will probably be a 'known' fish.

Stour (Kent)

Weight	Captor	Date
9lb 6oz	Carl Allman	June 2002

This tiny river flows through Canterbury, passing on through open marshland before emptying into Pegwell Bay. Carl Allman's fish was the first recorded of specimen size. In the same session he also caught barbel of 7lb 12oz and 6lb 4oz. The fish were caught near Kingsmead, Canterbury, using feeder-fished maggots.

Stour (Warwickshire)

Weight	Captor	Date
8lb 6oz	Nick Palmer	1989

This is a tributary of the Warwickshire Avon that joins the main river near Luddington below Stratford-upon-Avon. At Preston the river has depths to 13ft and is up to 45ft wide.

Nick Palmer a BCC member caught his fish 400yd from the mouth of the main river at Millcote in 1989. It was certainly not the largest barbel in the river but very little gets reported. A double-figure fish is still a possibility.

Swale (Yorkshire)

Weight	Captor	Date
12lb 12½oz	Brian Barton	Oct 1991
12lb 3oz	Gordon Booth	Dec 1999
12lb 2oz	John Schofield	Aug 2003

Rising above the village of Keld in Swaledale, the river runs for over 70 miles through some of the most beautiful scenery in Yorkshire, joining the Ure below the village of Myton.

The river has received a number of stockings. In 1991–92 some 9,000 fingerlings were introduced, followed in February 1997 by 3,000 12in fish and in April 1998 by another 3,000 small barbel. Autumn 1999 saw 2,000 fish added, with another 1,000 small barbel released in April 2002 into various Swale tributaries.

Brian Barton's fish was caught at Asenby Island, and, while photographs were taken and made available to the angling press, they were never published. This fish had been caught five or six times over a 3 years period with its weight fluctuating from 11lb upwards. A 13lb barbel caught by Martin Shaw of Knaresborough in September 1992 appeared to be the same fish as Barton's and, although considered a genuine capture, evidence was not provided.

Gordon Booth's barbel (*Angling Times*, photo of 15 December 1999) involved him driving some 50,000 miles over 25 years to fulfil his ambition of a double figure barbel. The fish measured 29in × 17½in and was also shown in the *Coarse Angling Today* magazine for February 2003.

Doubts surrounded the published photograph of Ted Harrison's 13lb 2oz November 2003 barbel as it was recognized as a fish caught recently at just over 9lb! The photograph in the *Anglers Mail*, 6 December 2003, was unconvincing. John Schofield's 12lb fish was witnessed by Steve Longmire and was tempted on meat (Photo *Angler's Mail*, 19 August 2003).

Taff (Wales)

Weight	Captor	Date
14lb 8oz	Justin Henwood	Aug 2001
12lb 8oz	Dave Halewood	Feb 2003
12lb 6oz	Malcolm Clarke	Dec 2002

Barbel were stocked in 1992 although the river is more usually associated with trout and salmon. In the last couple of years, specimen barbel have been reported.

Fishing upstream of Western Avenue Bridge in Cardiff, Justin Henwood, a local angler, latched onto a tremendous barbel of 14lb 8oz beating the previous river record held by Dave Halewood.

A 14lb 4oz fish claimed by Kevin Farrell in September 2001 lacked photographic evidence.

A 15lb barbel appears to be on the cards in the next 2–3 seasons.

Teme

Weight	Captor	Date
14lb 2oz	Martin Bluck	June 1994
13lb 12oz	Tom Cockfield	Oct 1987
13lb 9oz	L. Breakspear	Oct 1994

Barbel spread from the stockings into the river Severn in the 1950s. Huge fish were seen during electro-fishing surveys, with unconfirmed reports of a near 18lb barbel in 1994 that was returned to the river near Worcester. Probably a 'traveller' from the river Severn.

Martin Bluck's record fish was caught on meat in June 1994 at Bransford, beating the previous record by 6oz. Several 12- and low 13-pounders are caught most seasons, but it is difficult to see where a fish in the 16lb-18lb class is going to come from.

Top spots are Ham Hill, Bransford, Knightwick and Broadwas.

Thames

Weight	Captor	Date
14lb 13oz	Ted Bryan	Feb 2003
14lb 11oz	Ted Bryan	Jan 2003
(above entries are the same fish)		
14lb 2oz	Graham Elliott	Nov 2002
14lb 2oz	Dick Downing	Nov 2002

The mighty Thames has been a river in decline for over twenty years, often put down to the increase in boat traffic, erosion of spawning grounds and the most recently introduced American crayfish. Who actually put these into our rivers? These added to the problems of actually presenting a bait to the barbel.

The Environment Agency introduced 7,500 small barbel in late 2001, each marked with dye between Marlow and Kingston – considered by the Agency as ideal spawning grounds.

A 14lb 8oz fish credited to Lloyd Stone in July 1961 was returned to the river without proper verifications, and a 14lb 4oz fish caught in 1908 by R. Jones at Radcot Bridge came with no supporting evidence.

A 14-year-old schoolboy, Warren Healey, claimed a river record in September 1995, with a fish of 14lb 15oz, the *Angler's Mail* providing a photograph and report. However, local anglers questioned the weight of this fish claiming it was nearer 12lb. Certainly the photograph published appeared distorted and, as a result of the controversy raised, the fish was not considered as a genuine capture.

In July 1992 a 15lb 6oz barbel, credited to Ian Houston of Didcot, fishing at Long Wittenham during a night session, had no supporting evidence. Turning his attention from carp to barbel paid off for Ted Bryan. It resulted in a 14lb 11oz fish from the main river around the Oxford area in January 2003. Ted recaught the fish the following month at 14lb 13oz using Richworth boilies.

This fish breaks the old accepted Thames record of 14lb 6oz caught by T. Wheeler from Moseley in 1888, when there were doubts concerning the weighing procedures and firm evidence of capture was lacking. Graham Elliott's 14lb 2oz fish, in November 2002, was also caught on the main river, and appeared in the *Coarse Angling Today* magazine in May 2003. Graham's friend Dick Downing also caught a barbel at the same weight in the same month.

Trent

Weight	Captor	Date
15lb 2oz	Tim Ridge	Feb 2004
15lb 1oz	Alan Hughes	July 2003
15lb ½oz	Kenneth Clower	Oct 1999
14lb 13oz	Craig Woolhouse	July 2003
14lb 11oz	Steve Withers	Oct 2002

The mighty Trent began to suffer with pollution at the start of the Industrial

Ken Clower with his 15lb ½oz barbel caught on 19 October 1999. Ken held the river record for four years with this fish that had been tempted by the angler's own formula paste.

Revolution. However, even by 1900 it was still a tremendous fishery, with William Bailey, Frederick W.K. Wallis, Henry Coxon, J.W. Martin (Trent Otter) and their contemporaries having caught many specimens.

However, at the turn of the century the rot set in with a vengeance and the decline was rapid, with much pollution coming from major cities such as Nottingham. By the end of the 1914–18 war, it was ruined and became little more than an open sewer.

There is a general belief that with the cooling towers pumping warm water back into the river during the 1960s–70s, and a general clean-up of water quality, barbel and chub thrived. Now, with the cooling towers no longer operating, barbel have become much more localized, the cormorants decimating the smaller fish of the species.

For nearly four years, famous Nottingham angler Ken Clower held the river record. Even this fish did not come to light until a club publicity ban was partially lifted, allowing fish to appear in the March 2003 issue of the *Coarse Angling Today* magazine.

Alan Hughe's fish was reported in the *Angler's Mail*, 19 July 2003, together with a photograph. The same paper claimed a river record a week before with a fish caught by Steve Valente at 16lb 8oz. Unfortunately no one believed the weight claimed, several well-known river regulars stating that the fish would be pushed to make 11lb! Certainly with the controversy that this fish raised it could not be considered as a river record.

Craig Woolhouse's fish featured in the *Angler's Mail* and came from a swim near Newark, caught on a boilie.

Steve Withers had plenty of witnesses during a Barbel Catchers' Club fish in at Collingham. It was his first outing on the river, the fish weighing 14lb 11oz and a photograph was shown in the *Coarse Angling Today* magazine.

Tim Ridge banked the biggest authenticated barbel at 15lb 2oz after some 30 trips. He followed up with fish of 10lb 7oz and 9lb 4oz. The fish was very short and stocky. Home-made boilie on a Sufix Stealth Skin Trace was the successful method.

A fish of 16lb 4oz considered in the Nottingham area as a genuine fish was landed at Sawley by an unnamed Sheffield angler in 2001–02. No further details are available as the angler involved allegedly shuns publicity.

Collingham, Stoke Bardolph, Gunthorpe, East Stoke and Holme Marsh are all top spots. References to captures of large fish from Dunham Bridge are mainly false, these captures having come from higher upstream, usually from the Collingham AA water or the opposite bank. A 15lb 10oz fish claimed in 1999 remains unconfirmed. Certainly the river's first genuine 17lb fish cannot be far away.

Ure (Yorkshire)

Weight	Captor	Date
10lb 15oz	Martin Meechan	July 2003
10lb 13oz	Pete Riley	Oct 2001

Below Boroughbridge, close to the A1, much of the river tends to be slow and deep; this part of the river produces 8lb+ fish most seasons, but double-figure fish remain elusive. Higher up, the river is considerably shallower, and barbel are present, although they tend to be localized. Well-known spots are Boroughbridge, Ripon, Middleham and Tanfield.

In 1994, writer Bill Winship wrote passionately about Norris Sturdy's Yorkshire record barbel. Claimed at 14lb 4oz it would have been just 2oz short of the then national record. Caught at the tail end of the weir at Tanfield, no supporting photograph or evidence was provided and the fish was not reported to the angling press. Well-known Yorkshire angler Brian Moreland, also claimed a number of monster Ure barbel. In 1975, he reported to the *Angling Times* a catch of fish weighing 11lb 7oz, 10lb 6oz, 10lb 3oz, 10lb 1oz and 9lb 2oz taken over seven days on the middle reaches. Only a photograph of a 9lb fish ever appeared in print. The following year (April 1976), he further claimed a 14lb 5oz fish (beating the then existing British record by 9oz) when he was trout fishing. Again, no photographic evidence was available, although he claimed to have signed statements from two farmworkers.

Martin Meechan, a BCC member, caught his fish in July 2003 with photographs being made available, the fish having been witnessed. Pete Riley's fish was caught in a match and weighed on match scales. (*Angling Times*, 9 October 2001).

Wear

Weight	Captor	Date
12lb 2oz	Bob Gascoigne	Sept 1999
11lb 4oz	Chris Garner	Oct 2003

Barbel stocks in the river appear to be down to the illegal movement of fish from the Yorkshire rivers, but details remain sketchy. The river record won a Drennan Cup award, with photographs published in several magazines. Very few specimen barbel have been reported, but with the latest designer baits being used by specialist anglers this could soon change.

Bob Gascoigne's river record was shown in several angling publications having been caught on feeder fished casters.

Durham angler Chris Garner had his 11lb 4oz fish witnessed by Andy Burden and featured in a photograph in the *Angler's Mail* of 11 October 2003.

Best spots are around the Durham, Croxdale, Chester Moor and Maiden Castle areas. A 12lb 5oz fish received a mention in the press, but with no photographic evidence.

Welland (Lincolnshire)

Weight	Captor	Date
9lb 8oz	Al Taylor	Sept 1966

With some fast flows and gravelly bottom in parts, the river offers perfect spawning grounds for barbel.

The Environment Agency stocked some 2,500 barbel of around 6oz each into the river at Deeping St James in November 1998, with a further 2,000 fish of 6in released around Stamford in December 2001.

Al Taylor's fish was reported in the press (4 September 1966) with a photograph, but it may be several years before double-figure barbel become a regular feature. However, the signs are encouraging!

Wensum (Norfolk)

Weight	Captor	Date
17lb 1oz	Tim Ellis	Oct 2003
16lb 6oz	Stephen Keer	Aug 1998
15lb 13oz	Darren Gladden	Aug 2003

In 1972, 1990 and 1991, there were stockings of barbel throughout the river system, with the Wensum Action Group and the Norfolk Anglers Conservation Association (NACA) redefining the river at Lyng after the devastation caused by the local water authority with their dredging programmes.

With these stockings now producing double-figure barbel again, this must be put down as one of the country's success stories, where a group of individuals have fought long and hard since the 1980s to put the river back on the barbel map.

During 1972, a small stocking of river Severn barbel introduced below Costessey established themselves well enough to produce double-figure barbel by the 1980s. However, an increase in water abstraction later in the 1980s resulted in a decline in their numbers.

Stephen Keer, a Norwich schoolteacher held the UK barbel record with his 16lbs 6oz fish known as 'Red Belly'. Various anglers caught this same fish at fluctuating weights, the earliest capture being Dave Livermore's old river record at 15lb 9oz in October 1995. These fish were caught at Taverham Mill, although Costessey produced large specimens in the 1980s.

A surprise capture of a barbel claimed at 16lb 13oz in October 1998 caused huge controversy. The fish would have become a national record, but weighing irregularities ruled this out when it was thought that the fish had been weighed in a plastic bag with water in it. The captor, John Fulton, from Friern Barnet, London, a converted carp angler, failed to claim the river or national records because of the controversy.

News filtered through of several large barbel being caught off the river in the summer of 2003, the best being a new river record to Tim Ellis at 17lb 1oz during October 2003. Swimfeeder tactics combined with pellet hook-baits proved the successful method. Some rain had resulted in a little extra water coming through and Tim chose a normally productive swim, introducing feed via a bait dropper, before casting out his pellet hook-bait.

Within a short time his rod pulled round leaving him attached to a very large fish. As the fish was drawn into the net it was recognized as a known specimen having a missing left pectoral fin. Steve Loades and Tim's brother were called out to take photographs and witness the weight of 17lb 2ozs on the 'Avon' scales, later confirmed as 17lb 1oz after a scales check.

The river is recovering some of its former glory, due to the ten years' hard work of the Norfolk Anglers Conservation Association, who have carried out both major habitat restoration – including re-instatement of gravel riffles and bankside vegetation, river channel re-profiling and the actual stocking of fingerling barbel. Their efforts have set up a blue-print for river restoration, and it is hoped that other groups will follow their excellent example.

Wey (Surrey)

Weight	Captor	Date
14lb 5oz	Steve King	Feb 2001
13lb 8oz	Steve Carden	March 1999
12lb 13oz	Dave Ball	March 1998

The tiny river Wey is a 25-mile-long tributary of the Thames, winding its way through the beautiful countryside of West Surrey. Eleven pound and 12lb fish are not uncommon but have to be worked hard for, most of the fish coming at night.

Steve King's fish was a genuine capture, being witnessed by two well-known anglers, but the Byfleet Club has imposed a strict publicity ban so no photographs were released to the press.

Steve Carden's March 1999 fish is a genuine specialist group (BCC) capture. Dave Ball's fish, reported together with a photo in March 1998, was the best barbel recorded at the time, since Jason Bailey's nationally disputed record of 15lb 12oz back in August 1990. The capture of a 14lb 11oz barbel remains unconfirmed.

The river appears to fish best late in the season, with high water or flood conditions prevailing. Specimens have been caught at Abbey Stream, Addlestone and the old Woking stretch.

Regular specialist on the river, Steve Carden captured a huge specimen at 14lb 2oz in November 2002 (photograph: *Barbel Rivers and Captures*), this fish being just 3oz under the river record. Having set off for home after a blank session on the river, he decided to avoid the rush-hour traffic by diverting to another part of the river for a couple of hours. Fishing a weir pool, the specimen was safely netted having fallen for a hair-rigged HNV Bait.

Wharfe (Yorkshire)

Weight	Captor	Date
13lb 2oz	James Illingworth	Autumn 2003
12lb 12oz	Tony Rocca	Sept 2003
12lb 10oz	Mick Wood	Sept 2003
12lb 2oz	Mick Wood	June 2004

Rising on Carn Fell, the river leaves the Yorkshire Dales at Bolton Abbey, flowing down through the towns of Ilkley and Otley before finally joining the River Ouse at Cawood. Popular spots are Harewood Weir, Linton, Boston Spa, Newton Kyme and Ulleskelf.

James Illingworth's fish is not only the river record but the largest barbel caught in Yorkshire. It was witnessed by Duncan Mellors and another local specialist angler.

Tony Rocca's first Yorkshire barbel turned out to be the river record at the time of capture, falling for a maggot feeder approach by the North Lincolnshire angler.

One of the most successful barbel anglers on the river is Tadcaster based Mick Wood, with a string of 11lb plus fish

to his name. A 14lb fish in a year or two remains a realistic possibility although a number of recaptures do occur.

Windrush (Oxfordshire)

Weight	Captor	Date
11lb 9oz	Danny Empson	June 1998

A small picturesque tributary of the river Thames, the Windrush flows through the Cotswold countryside and has suffered in recent years through destructive abstraction, reducing the river to a sluggish brook in places. Despite this, it can still suffer from flooding when the main river overflows in winter.

Specialist anglers have formed action groups to lobby the Environment Agency and local MPs and hopefully the river will be allowed to return to its former glory.

Danny Empson, using a Pulse rod, targeted the tiny river and captured the fishery record in June 1998. The *Angler's Mail* referred to this capture.

With so few reports received on barbel of specimen size, this record may stand for some time.

Witham (Lincolnshire)

Weight	Captor	Date
9lb 14oz	Colin Wilson	March 2000

In 1994, 1,000 barbel were stocked at Foston, near Grantham, with a further 1,000 introduced near Lincoln in December 1995.

A barbel of 14lb 10oz was claimed by Nottingham schoolboy Matt Walters in October 2003 having been reported in the *Angling Times* as the river record. On checking with the paper it was stated that 'the fish had been photographed in a landing net and was more likely to be around 8lbs!'

Wye

Weight	Captor	Date
14lb 9oz	Mike Easton	July 2003
14lb 9oz	Tim Joyce	Nov 2000
13lb 10oz	Len Bowers	Oct 1998

Flowing from Builth Wells through Hereford down to Chepstow, the Wye is a majestic river. For many years it was highly regarded as a game river, but with declining salmon stocks, sections of the river have been opened up for coarse anglers, with the emphasis on chub and barbel. The Red Lion stretch at Bredwardine has long been known as a barbel area, with Fownhope, Hay and Hereford being other favoured stretches.

Herefordshire angler Mike Easton had spent forty years trying to catch a double-figure barbel – and then had three in one day! Fish of 11lb 2oz, 12lb 1oz and 14lb 9oz all fell to meat baits. The largest fish equalled the previously claimed river record by Tim Joyce caught in November 2000. However, doubts were cast on the weight of Joyce's fish after a photograph was published in the *Angler's Mail* of 11 November 2000.

Several claims of 17lb fish being caught by salmon anglers have lacked any photographic evidence although the river undoubtedly holds fish far larger than the current record.

Yare (Norfolk)

Weight	Captor	Date
10lb 1oz	Chris Turnbull	Jan 2000

This is a surprisingly long river that flows from near East Dereham through Norwich, where the Wensum briefly joins it at Thorpe Station before winding its way into the sea at Great Yarmouth. The upper reaches contain specimen barbel, but few are ever reported.

A photograph of Chris Turnbull's excellent fish featured in the *Coarse Angling Today* magazine in March 2003.

A fish credited to Kevin Matthews at 10lb 12oz in October 2001 lacked any photographic evidence, but is considered by many to be the river's best barbel.

Barbel may stray from the Wensum so an 11lb+ fish may be a possibility.

POSTSCRIPT –
1 DECEMBER 2004

In order to meet the publication deadline, the section containing the stories behind the capture of the largest specimens from each river had to be set at 16 June 2004.

During the first few months of the new season (2004–5) eighteen river records were broken and the country's first-ever 20lb barbel landed. To record these important events and to present an up-to-date picture as possible, a revised river listing has been drawn up at 1 December 2004 and is shown at the end of the section. This provided an interesting comparison with the 16 June listing and illustrates how rapidly the barbel scene is changing.

Barbel UK River Records as at 1 December 2004

	River	Weight lb oz	Date	Captor	Potential Weight lb
1	Anker (Staffs)	10 02	Sept 2003	Sean Allison	11
2	Arun (Sussex)	11 02	Nov 2003	Brian Ayling	12
3	Arrow (Warks)	12 02	Oct 2004	Mick Harris	14
4	Avon (Bristol)	15 09½	Feb 1998	Stuart Morgan	17
5	Avon (Hampshire)	15 07	Oct 2004	Will Ward	17
6	Avon (Warks)	15 14	July 2004	David Wren	17
7	Blackwater (Berks)	11 04	Aug 1999	Bob Vince	12
8	Cherwell (Oxon)	13 00	Oct 2002	Mick Coleman	14
9	Colne (Middlesex)	15 05	Jan 2002	Paul Jebb	16
10	Colnebrook	8 01	Oct 1991	Andy Harman	10
11	Coppermill Stream	11 06	Oct 1992	David Poole	12
12	Dane (Cheshire)	14 04	Aug 1994	Phil Booth	15
13	Derwent (Derbys)	12 11	Nov 2003	Jamie Alexander	14
14	Derwent (Yorks)	12 06	Sept 1989	Jon Wolfe	13
15	Don (Yorks)	8 04	Sept 2002	Christian Lawrence	10
16	Dove (Staffs)	15 12	Sept 2004	Steve Stayner	17
17	Drapers Osier Bed	7 02	Aug 2000	Jim Knight	10
18	Ember (Surrey)	9 04	Aug 2001	Seb Pizzuto	11
19	Frome (Somerset)	12 12	July 2004	Jonathan George	14
20	Holybrook	13 04	Oct 2003	Trevor King	14
21	Ivel (Beds)	14 04	Nov 2004	Paul Webb	16
22	Kennet (Berks)	17 02	Oct 2004	Paul Smythe	19
23	Lea	15 12	Oct 2004	Terry Ettridge	17
24	Leam (Warks)	11 09	Mar 2000	Trevor Kennedy	12
25	Loddon (Berks)	16 10	Nov 2004	Duncan Charman	17
26	Lugg (Hereford)	10 08	July 1999	Darren Godsall	11
27	Mease (Staffs)	13 00	Nov 1996	Phil Hart	14
28	Medway (Kent)	16 02	June 1994	Pete Woodhouse	17
29	Mole (Surrey)	13 05	Jan 2003	Paul Starkey	15
30	Nene (Northants)	13 00	Summer 2002	Duncan Kay	14
31	Nidd (Yorks)	11 04	Oct 1993	Phil Johnson	12
32	Ouse, Great*	20 06	Oct 2004	Tony Gibson	23
33	Ouse (Sussex)	11 08½	Oct 2000	Kevin Colston Iles	12
34	Ouse (Yorks)	11 10	Sept 2004	Darren Starkey	13
35	Potts Stream (Oxon)	13 08	Oct 1968	John Ginifer	–
36	Ribble (Lancs)	14 09	Nov 2004	Mark Birchall	16
37	Rother (Sussex)	12 12	Jan 2004	Pete Foster	14
38	St Patricks Stream	15 08	Oct 2001	Keith Evans	16
39	Severn	16 03	Nov 1997	Howard Maddocks	17
40	Soar (Leics)	12 07	Sept 2004	G Stadden	13
41	Sow (Staffs)	10 00½	Sept 2002	Stewart Bloor	11

Barbel UK River Records as at 1 December 2004 (continued)

	River	Weight lb oz	Date	Captor	Potential Weight lb
42	Stour (Dorset)	16 02	Feb 2003	Graham Sale	17
43	Stour (Kent)	9 06	June 2002	Carl Allman	10
44	Stour (Warks)	8 06	1989	Nick Palmer	10
45	Swale (Yorks)	13 04	Oct 2004	Rob Parsons	14
46	Taff (Wales)	14 08	Aug 2003	Justin Henwood	15
47	Teme	14 02	June 1994	Martin Bluck	15
48	Tees	12 11	Aug 2004	Peter Tietsh	14
49	Thame	9 12	2001	John Sheldon	10
50	Thames	17 12	Nov 2004	Wes Thomas	19
51	Trent	15 02	Feb 2004	Tim Ridge	18
52	Ure (Yorks)	10 15	July 2003	Martin Meechan	11
53	Wear (Durham)	12 07	Sept 2004	Nigel Collins	13
54	Welland (Lincs)	9 08	Sept 1966	Al Taylor	10
55	Wensum (Norfolk)	17 14	Autumn 2004	Stephen Harper	19
56	Wey (Surrey)	14 05	Feb 2001	Steve King	16
57	Wharfe (Yorks)	14 04	Nov 2004	Steve Hill	16
58	Windrush (Oxon)	11 09	June 1998	Danny Empson	12
59	Witham (Lincs)	9 14	Mar 2000	Colin Wilson	10
60	Wye	14 09	July 2003	Mike Easton	16
61	Yare (Norfolk)	10 01	Jan 2000	Chris Turnbull	11

*Present national record.

INDEX

INDEX